The
Prosperous
Gardener

The Prosperous Gardener

A Guide to Gardening the Organic Way

by James Jankowiak

Illustrations by Daryl Hunter

 Rodale Press Emmaus, PA

Printed in the United States of America
on recycled paper.

Library of Congress Cataloging in Publication Data

Jankowiak, James.
   The prosperous gardener.

   Bibliography: p.
   Includes index.
   1. Vegetable gardening.   2. Organic gardening.
3. Fruit-culture.   I. Title.
SB324.3J36   635'.04'8   77-18089
ISBN 0-87857-204-7

2 4 6 8 10 9 7 5 3 1

To my parents, Edwin and Louise Jankowiak,
whose love and faith sustained me.

Contents

Contents

Contents

Acknowledgments

I want to give special thanks in particular to a few of the many people who helped, taught, and advised me in the art of writing, the craft of gardening, and the way of abundant living.

To Stephen Fish, invaluable friend, advisor, and co-worker; to Tom Becotte, Paul LaMontaigne, and Jim Boutcher, who bore the weight of many of my experiments; to Robert L. Scott, who taught me much about writing through word and example; to Jerome Goldstein, Maury Franz, Carol Stoner, and Lori Breslow of Rodale Press, who suggested this book, worked with it, and encouraged me; to Jim and Dacie Durkin, parents in Jesus Christ; and to my wife, Lynn, who endured muddy feet in the living room and weeds in the kitchen, and still loves me.

Introduction:
Nature Cares

Gardening is an affair of the heart. It's that simple. When we care for our vegetables and flowers—do the sowing, weeding, thinning, cultivating, watering, fertilizing, and harvesting on time—they respond with beautiful growth and rich yields. When we neglect them they quickly take on an unkempt look and produce little food or beauty. Care makes the difference between the prosperous and poor garden.

That's what organic gardening and this book are all about—bringing out the best in our soil, flowers, fruits, and vegetables. That, in turn, will give us the best possible products to share with our families, friends, and animals. It's no small task. I offer it to you as a challenge to care: to care for the earth and to care for the living things that inhabit it.

We can do this by following the example of nature. Nature takes care of the earth by constantly replenishing and renewing it. I saw this clearly on a recent visit to the northern Illinois community where I grew up. There is a section of field there that eventually wore out because of continuous exploitive cropping. About fifteen or twenty years ago it was nearly a solid thistle patch. When the owners planted the rest of the field they went around that patch because it was so poor. This gave the thistles a chance to grow up and die unhindered season after season. When I saw it on this last trip a few thistles were still there, but a species of goldenrod had moved in, and so had grasses and a few shrubs. I would guess the entire patch will eventually turn back into an oak forest since that is what borders it on two sides. This is a good example of nature's attempt to repair the damage done by man's thoughtless use of the land.

The main difference between modern farming and

organic gardening is that the latter imitates nature by taking care to enrich the soil. In my first northern California garden I decided to put a garden alongside a stream on a slope of the logged-over land I then owned. I had to cut away a couple of fir trees, then I made rock

RENEWAL OF THE THISTLE PATCH

terraces, and finally I double-trenched the dirt behind the terraces. This was certainly an alteration of the environment, but the reason I chose the location was because it was an open spot in the forest. I didn't have to alter the environment too much and it offered a challenge to the organic method.

The soil itself was poor and gravelly in spots. To build it up I gathered leaf mold from the forest floor, purchased and spread agricultural dolomite to offset the soil acidity, and added rock phosphate and wood ashes. This was the human way to do quickly what nature does over the ages. I also mulched heavily with leaves and kelp that I had collected from the ocean. As I harvested the crops I either returned the part I didn't eat directly to the soil where the natural process of decaying and recycling could take place, or composted the materials with other vegetation or waste products I had gathered elsewhere to return to the soil.

The garden, through my care, became a beneficial part of nature. Friends and I ate the produce as did the forest animals from the deer and mice to lizards and birds. The formerly sparse soil was covered with growing things. After a couple of years there were thousands of earthworms where only a handful had existed. My homestead had an increased capacity for life, which when you think about it, is just another way of saying I took responsibility for my place in the environment in a way that benefited all living things.

I don't think you can separate a person from his work, which is why I started out saying care is what makes the garden. It also makes the gardener. The principles that I practice didn't come to me all at once, and perhaps by quickly tracing my own development as an organic gardener, you can see that it's practice that produces perfection.

I actually made my first attempt at planting when I was about five years old—I used to take prune and peach pits and cherry seeds and plant them in our Chicago backyard in the hope of growing more fruit. As I grew older and even more enthusiastic, I collected cottonwood, elm, and maple and started little plantations. When I was about ten I planted my first garden in a very unlikely place between two garages because the sunny part of the yard was in lawn or my grandmother's peonies. I grew radishes, carrots, kohlrabi, lettuce, and watermelon with very little understanding of plant or soil needs. But I cared for my plants and they responded as best they could.

Several years later we moved about fifty miles north of Chicago. I bought my first rifle and established my first trapline. I became interested in homesteading, having been influenced by stories I read in *Outdoors in Illinois* and *Wisconsin Agriculturist*. I built a worm bed, tapped maple trees, began collecting roots and leaves, and roamed the fields and woods for wild edibles— painstakingly learning almost everything by hard experience because nobody I knew had any homesteading knowledge. Eventually I got the idea to buy some land, and became an avid reader of the *Chicago Tribune's* "country property" Sunday classifieds, where ads touted Arkansas land for as low as two dollars an acre. My parents pointedly suggested I go to college first and think about land afterwards.

There's something about stark reality that can dampen even the most ambitious dreams. My first year of college was at the University of Illinois. I remember looking out my dorm window at winter-bleak rows of cold windswept corn and soybean stubble and thinking to myself, if this is what good farming is like, I'm in the wrong place. The idea of spending five years to get twin degrees in journalism and agriculture so I could be an effective agricultural extension worker blew away with the freezing north winds. (I do have to admit that lately I've come to appreciate the beauty of the Midwest heartland). The agricultural world seemed too big, too chemical, and too profit-oriented, and the flat prairie lands too dreary. I envisioned fish ponds with wildfowl food planted along their edges, big woodlots, a sugar bush, an orchard, and crops and livestock of every description. What I saw around me was monocropping and big single-species livestock operations. I felt like I needed a new direction, something that would lead me into a "closer to nature" approach to life, so I went to Hawaii to learn Asian and Pacific culture.

Through observation and study I discovered that the cultures of the Pacific and Asia had a high regard for land ownership, use, and care. The soil was not exploited, but lovingly cared for and passed on from generation to generation. By comparison a lot of American agriculture was more akin to the "slash and burn" techniques of primitive tribes than the refined techniques of many non-Western societies. While going to school and reflecting on all these things I worked a couple years for the University of Hawaii grounds department. Just about every gardener was an old Filipino or Japanese with a keen understanding of the details of ornamental gardening. The emphasis was on human skill rather than chemical methods, and it showed in beautiful flowers that were coaxed into fullest bloom, and in the generally neat grounds. What a contrast to the nearby agricultural experimental station with its "dangerous chemicals" warnings posted in front of crops.

Eventually I moved to California and got my first taste of starting a garden from ground zero. The shady backyard of the San Francisco Victorian I rented had been a depository for old tires, garbage, broken bottles, and tin cans for many years. I carried away the junk and what few weeds managed to grow in that abused environment and found a very poor sand soil. I brought in bales of peat moss and bags of composted steer manure. The newly enriched soil held respectable quantities of water, and I had a modest garden and a small lawn, both of which gave me satisfaction far beyond their size. It was becoming clear to me that it wasn't the quality of the

5

land with which you started that determined the success of your garden, but rather it was what you did with the land once you started working with it.

But turning near-worthless soil in San Francisco backyards into productive and pleasing gardens didn't exactly satisfy me. I still had the urge to homestead. I moved to suburban Marin County and got my first taste of California's famous adobe soil. It worked up well in the spring, but baked as hard as a brick in the 100° San Rafael sun, blasting many of my vegetables. The solution was mulch for the soil surface, and peat moss and sand underneath.

I still didn't really feel that I was "back to the land," though. So I scraped together all the capital I could and bought ninety-seven acres of land straddling the Mendocino-Humboldt county line within view of the northern California ocean. Now I was a homesteader! By choice there was no road into my property. Everything I needed from the "outside" came in on my back or was skidded in by human power. It was a good way to teach myself what was essential and what wasn't. I lived just on the edge of the fog zone in what I considered a nearly ideal cool weather climate. It was warm enough to grow corn, beans, tomatoes, and peppers outdoors in summer, and cool enough to grow leafy greens and cole crops year around. Frosts were light and didn't interfere with half-hardy crops.

At first I did everything by the book—Rodale's *How to Grow Vegetables and Fruits by the Organic Method*—but gradually I met old-time gardeners who taught me volumes just by the way they transplanted a tomato or pruned a grape vine. My neighbors were almost to a person organic homesteaders, and we pooled our knowledge and our aspirations. I began to develop the methods of optimum productivity that I share in this book.

My soil was basically poor and steep, covered by forest. It was hard work to bring it into vegetable production, so each piece had to do more than double duty. Besides that there was the task of house building and all the other endless details of living on the land. Though I had all the time in the world living out there in the woods free from the hustle of the city and the necessity of punching a timecard according to somebody else's hours, my time was limited because I had to budget so much for house building, so much for gardening, so much for the chickens, etc.

Space and time became two very precious tools. The more concentrated use I could make of each the better off I was. For example, I built a root crop bed that was terraced on two sides so I could work part of the crops standing up. This saved time. Since the soil was very rich, I could, by careful spacing, grow two to four times as much in one plot as by the normal row method. Less space meant developing less land for production, thereby saving time. And working in a concentrated space saved motions and even more time. It was a period of discovery for me. In the past I had always made my living working for other people. They provided management. Now the word "management" became a real part of my experience. Besides managing space and time, and my own inner determination to develop myself, I had to manage my stewardship of the earth so that it fit into the whole scheme of life.

After three years of living in comparative isolation, personal changes made me decide to move to Living Waters Ranch, a Christian community some eight or nine miles up the road from my place. Here I did reforestation work and learned how to harvest wild foliage. I barely got settled there when the call came for a gardener for the Lighthouse Ranch, another Christian community that at that time supported about 150 people. It was located in a former Coast Guard station on a bluff overlooking Humboldt Bay and the Pacific Ocean just south of Eureka. I volunteered and became chief gardener of about an acre of very good organic soil, with carte blanche to develop the three other good tillable acres as I saw fit. I had to train less experienced but aspiring gardeners, grow enough food to feed the community, and have some to give away to the area's needy. It was a real challenge.

That first spring I spied out all the sunniest and warmest locations on the windy, foggy promontory and planted them to warm weather crops. I got as much seed of varied strains of different species as I could and planted them in different sections to see what would and wouldn't work. I gathered seaweed and sawdust by the ton for mulches and composts. There was plenty of manure from chickens, pigs, cows, and occasionally sheep, goats, and rabbits. The cool weather crops, nutured by rich organic foods and lots of loving care and prayer, grew beyond my wildest expectations. The warm weather crops wouldn't make it except under glass or plastic.

There was room for experimentation everywhere. With sometimes fifteen people working in the garden I was able to guide them into labor-intensive, high-production techniques. I tried every method that promised fruitful possibilities; keeping a journal, and constantly refining what I already knew. Later, with my wife Lynn's help, I branched out from crops and herbs into houseplants and flowers. I figured the nursery and groundskeeping methods I had learned in Hawaii, translated into California terms and enlarged upon, would come in handy for teaching a trade to some of the people in the community, to say nothing of beautifying the grounds.

I also became friends at that time with Stephen Fish, who had received his agricultural training at Oregon State University. With his firsthand knowledge of the nonorganic side of farming, Steve convinced me there was much good in the way chemical farmers raised crops and grew livestock. Up to that time I had pretty much dismissed mainstream American agriculture as irrelevant. I started by reading a couple of high school vocational agriculture books and found out that underneath those shiny big tractors and half-day-long rows of wheat was a lot of growing savvy that, translated into organic terms, would make for better gardening. I began to keep up on the state farm journal and on Cooperative Extension Service publications. For example, the whole basis of my tomato pruning method is one worked out by University of Illinois agroscientists. I'm sure their aim was to assist the chemical growers, but that doesn't change the value of the method.

Coincidentally, a year later I became part of a group that agreed to pick apples for a large, chemically grown Washington orchard in return for wages, housing, and a place to hold meetings. The manager, Max Sikstrom, had been a tropical fruit and vegetable grower in Australia, a commercial tomato grower and sheep raiser in Canada, and now had his own apple, pear, and cherry orchard adjacent to the one we had contracted to pick. Max had developed his orchard out of virgin sagebrush into highly productive acreage by using innovative techniques such as central leader pruning, drip irrigation, and hedgerow spacing. We took a liking to one another, and because I was open to big scale agricultural methods (his orchard and the one he managed combined produced in excess of 225,000 bushels of fruit a year), Max was able to teach me many of the principles behind high-production tree pruning, drip irrigation, planting, picking, training, and labor relations. I got very adept at translating chemical requirements like so many pounds of nitrogen, phosphorus, and potassium per acre into tons of sludge or compost per acre as I considered how to change his operation over to organic. In the end, of course, I had to maintain my organic integrity.

Gardening that season in north central Washington was my first experience with organic methods in an area with distinct seasonal changes. I had plenty of opportunity to verify methods I had developed along the

California north coast, and also to increase my understanding of corn, bean, and tomato production. Most important, I had the chance to identify with most gardeners who have to work with continental instead of maritime climates. For the most part I found once I understood how to garden in one place I could easily move to another place and do the same thing with good results. There are, of course, regional variations in planting dates, best-suited varieties and strains of vegetables, soils, and rainfall differences, but they can all be learned in a matter of a few years through observation and practice.

Most recently I've been channeling my agricultural talents into extremely high-production raised-bed practices that can be easily taught and adapted to various climates, and which aren't dependent on a large cash outlay for land or equipment. My experiments aren't based on the latest scientific advances but on the intensive beds of the old Chinese gardeners and on the terraces of the Hawaiian taro planters I studied when I was looking for that "closer to nature" lifestyle during my college days.

Right now I'm working with about ten acres of clay soil in a river valley just south of Eureka. The land is all on the slopes, not on the bottoms. Some is covered with scrub, some is suitable for livestock. Before a small group of us started to rework it organically none of it was really suitable for vegetable cropping, so it's become a sort of showpiece for what manpower plus organic ingenuity can do to make food available on a consistent, wholesome basis. Taking my cue from the terraced beds of the Oriental experts, borrowing heavily from current organic practices, and making full use of whatever I can of modern scientific agriculture and vegetable strains, I'm terracing the ground and making planting beds, greenhouses, and year-around growing cold frames. Though I could come in with a D8 Caterpillar tractor I've preferred to work mainly by hand to get the feel of how effective my methods would be in a remote village in Guatemala or in somebody's backyard in Seattle.

In the chapters that follow I'll detail ways you can make your own piece of ground a productive farm or garden while replenishing the land through natural methods. These ways are not pie-in-the-sky or some fad. They mean good, hard, honest work which will bear the fruit of good health. None of the principles of gardening in this book will turn a garden into Eden in a season, but patiently and carefully applied, they'll produce more and more bountiful results as the years pass.

PART I:
Gardening Basics

1
Water:
Lifeblood of the Garden

When I moved to northern California practically the first words my nearest neighbor Jay Sooter said to me one dusty July afternoon were, "I hope you've got good springs." When I asked him why, he proceeded to tell me that it had only rained around there once since the previous February 12.

It didn't rain again until October, and although I recorded 125 inches over the next six months, the rains stopped in April, and except for a few light showers, didn't resume again until the following October. In southern coastal California the season is even shorter, from about mid-December until mid-March, and by the time you get out to Nevada and Arizona, rains are a novelty at the lower elevations.

It's no wonder I've come to regard water as the lifeblood of the soil. I can't afford to take it for granted. You can grow plants with water and no soil, but you can't grow plants with soil and no water. It's sometimes hard for gardeners east of the Mississippi to realize, since so many important agricultural products come from the West, but over the intermountain and West Coast states the major rainfall comes in the winter and it often doesn't amount to much.

That means that the huge vegetable, fruit, cotton, and hay-growing areas of California, the nation's biggest volume and value agricultural producer, would be mostly sagebrush and desert if it wasn't for one thing— irrigation. In the western states, with the possible exceptions of coastal Washington and northwestern Oregon, most people depend on irrigation either from locally available springs, wells, creeks, government irrigation projects, or—most expensively—municipal water supplies.

Even in the East, it's necessary to irrigate from time to time. My folks, who usually make out well with normal rainfall plus a few supplementary waterings in their northern Illinois garden, made the decision to turn their crops over to the whims of nature in a recent extremely dry season. They felt their metered municipal water was too costly to use. I was in their garden that August. The zucchinis had stopped growing, the winter squashes were perhaps a third their normal size, the peppers looked like buttons, and the tomatoes that had set earlier in the season, though mature, were small and misshapen. It was obvious that no tomatoes would mature on those vines in the coming months.

I think the message is clear: The person who builds a garden around a water supply will be the one who escapes the pain of seeing crops dry up in drought or new transplants shrivel in unexpected heat. Check out your water supply carefully to make sure that even in dry years it's adequate to irrigate the vegetables you grow. I know people who have decided on a garden location or planted fruit trees with no regard to the availability or cost of water. I know others who bought land in the winter or early spring when water was running in seemingly strong creeks only to find out in summer that their crops dried up with those same creeks.

Watering—the Right Way

I particularly want to emphasize the need for good cheap water or an efficient way to apply expensive water because, with the exception of neglect, improper watering is probably the greatest reason for failure in the small garden. Most inexperienced gardeners probably believe there's no real trick to watering—you just do it. But if you know how water works in the soil, you realize there's a right way—and a wrong way—to water.

Watering would be a breeze if the soil would only

remain at what is known as field capacity, a state of
equilibrium in which the water content is uniform
throughout the soil. At field capacity every soil particle
and every bit of humus is holding the maximum amount
of water, which means that the water is moving neither
upward nor downward.

HOW WATER WORKS IN THE SOIL

When the soil is at field capacity it's not only moist, but is also well aerated—conditions under which plants thrive. If the water would only stay that way until it is used by the plant, gardeners would have far less work to do. But what happens almost immediately is the drier atmosphere draws on the soil moisture and it goes into the air as vapor, just the way wet clothes dry on a line. As the air removes water from the soil particles nearest the surface, capillary action draws water from lower particles in an attempt to maintain the equal distribution of water. (This water loss can be stopped by the right application of mulches, as I'll explain later.)

While all this is going on, the plant is pulling water into its system by the process of osmosis. Through a second process called transpiration, additional water is being drawn into the atmosphere from the soil through the plant's roots, up its stem, and out its leaves. This is setting up great pressure in the plant so that it's acting something like a pump to move water out of the soil. But if the plant doesn't have enough power to pull any more water it wilts (although it still continues to transpire). If the situation isn't corrected, the plant first stops growing and then it withers and dies.

Since it takes between 200 and 900 pounds of water to make 1 pound of dry vegetable matter, it's easy to understand why all plants need thorough watering— preferably with soft rainwater that's as close as possible to the air temperature. My opinion is that the soil should be wetted to a depth of twelve inches for all deep-rooted crops; and for all shallow-rooted crops like lettuce, eight inches.

There is some question as to how much of the soil should dry out before repeating a watering cycle. My rule in the past was to irrigate when the top inch dried out. Lately I've been thinking that one inch is good for deep-rooted, established crops, but a half-inch is best for most other crops. The exceptions are a few of the fast growers like lettuce and radishes which I now water when the topsoil shows signs of drying. (If you have a mulch over the soil and it dries out, that's alright. It's only when the topsoil becomes dry that I recommend watering.)

I've also discovered that just as too little water is unhealthy for plants, so is too much. Whenever the moisture content of the soil is at the saturation level there's no room for gasses to move in and out of the root zone. Noxious gasses, the by-products of the life process, will poison a plant if they can't be released into the air. Also, when the roots are in water the plant can't get enough oxygen to breathe and it may "drown." Finally, if the water table is close to the soil surface, plant roots have a very limited field in which to grow and gather nutrients and plant size is stunted. Often raised beds or drainage tile can correct this problem.

Assuming you have good drainage or are on the way to building it, how you get water to your plants will be the most important consideration in your total watering plan. As I see it, the objective is to give the plants all the water they need for growth without leaching any nutrients from the soil and without having so much water in the ground that air flow is impaired. A good irrigation system should accomplish all those things.

Setting Up an Irrigation System

The first two questions you'll have to deal with in setting up an irrigation system is where your water will be coming from and how it will be stored.

If I had my druthers, I'd druther have a gravity-flow irrigation system with storage tanks supplied by springs or wells on my land. With a gravity-flow system there's no need for any kind of mechanical power to get the water from where it flows to where you want it. For instance, on land I owned in Whale Gulch, California, there was a spring about two hundred feet vertically

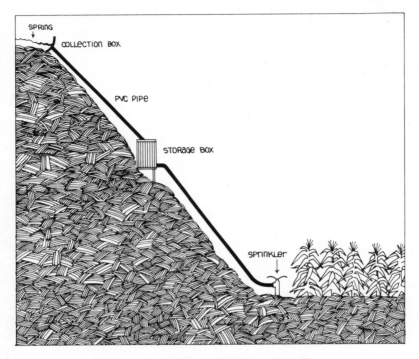

WHALE GULCH IRRIGATION SYSTEM

above the garden on the side of a hill. All I had to do was fill a reservoir and that provided enough pressure to turn sprinklers.

My second choice would be a deep well with a nearby elevated storage tank high enough and big enough to operate sprinklers. At the Lighthouse Ranch we had a storage tank with a pump that pumped water into a water tower. From there it flowed on demand as the vertical drop provided the needed pressure. An electric triggering device turned on the pump whenever the water tower was two-thirds empty.

I should point out that in both cases the water source was on my land. Any other way, someone else is in direct control of availability and that always translates "more expense."

20

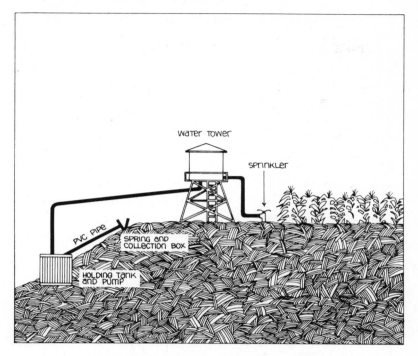

water tower

sprinkler

PVC PIPE

SPRING and
COLLECTION BOX

HOLDING Tank
and PUMP

LIGHTHOUSE RanCH IrrigaTion SysTem

The final question is how to deliver the water. I've tried several methods and have settled on overhead sprinkling and drip irrigation.

I use pulsating and oscillating sprinklers and find that properly installed and operated, the water sinks into the soil like a gentle rain, does not cause puddling, and does not damage seedbeds. Pulsators, sprinklers in which the heads travel in a complete circle a few degrees at a time, are good for tall crops like corn and sunflowers when mounted on poles six to ten feet high. Oscillators, which have heads that move from left to right and back again, suffice for lower growing crops and seedbeds. A few of either type and a good flexible hose will cover most gardens. I get the best coverage by laying out the sprinklers at the apexes of equilateral triangles instead of down the rows in a rectangular pattern.

The first sprinkler system I built was simple in the extreme. I dug out a spring, making a collection box lined with rocks to gather the water and act as a filter. Just above the bottom of the box was the drain end of PVC (polyvinylchloride) pipe that led in from beneath. We were careful that the pipe was not right on the bottom of the box or else it would have constantly picked up sediment, leaves, and sticks. This way the impurities settled out and the clear water flowed into the reservoir. (If this sounds a little confusing, think of the collection box as a kitchen sink. The water goes from the spring or creek [water faucet] into the collection box [sink]. Just as the sink has a drain that leads the water through the pipes, so does the collection box. The only difference is that the drain is a couple of inches above the bottom of the box rather than on the bottom.) My first storage tank was nothing more than a garbage can donated by a neighbor. Its capacity was too small to turn a sprinkler but it worked fine with a nozzle at the end of a hose.

Later, in a community garden I helped develop, we put in a similar system. PVC pipe (rated for drinking) carried water from a collection box to a 1,000-gallon metal tank that we placed 100 or so feet higher up the side of a mountain than the garden was. An overflow on the top of the tank led excess water back into the spring bed. We used PVC pipe to lead the water into the garden and buried the pipe the full length of the center paths. The system also had moveable hoses and pulsating sprinkler heads which rimmed the garden at a height of about 6 feet.

I brought a friend to see the garden one particularly hot day. Most of the surrounding land was brown and dry, but the garden was lush like a jungle with tall corn, berry vines, huge tomato plants, New Zealand spinach, and sunflowers. The garden itself was in the proverbial middle of nowhere, almost unseen from the road, not near any houses, and many miles from the nearest town. It seemed like a special oasis. As we walked through the deer-proof fence, my friend, who was quite taken by such an impressive layout in such a remote location, jokingly said, "The only thing you're missing here is a golf course watering system." I walked over and turned on the main valve and suddenly a rainlike spray began falling on the garden. It was a pretty striking sight—and it cost under $100.

Drip Irrigation

Gravity flow also works with drip irrigation, a system which uses soaker hoses to slowly apply water directly to plant roots. Drip irrigation is a boon to folks who have to pay to have their water brought from a distance or who go on vacation frequently during the growing season and don't have anyone to care for their crops. By delivering water through very small openings in tubes called emitters, drip irrigation puts water where it's needed and nowhere else at a substantial savings over conventional overhead sprinkling systems.

Drip opens land for bush and tree crops that was formerly thought to be too steep as well as making economical gardening possible in fertile desert areas. You can control the amount of water going to each type of crop through valves, different size hoses, distance from the water main, or all three. With drip it's possible to rig up ways to feed plants with fish emulsions, manure teas, or other fertilizers at the same time you water. (Simply place them in a pressure tank, figure the total flow from the tank, the average water flow from the emitters, and make the correct dilution.) The fertilizer goes into the root system without any waste, and although the liquid fertilizer option is available in an overhead system, too, the fertilizer is broadcast rather than concentrated.

Drip, of course, does have its drawbacks. Although it's good for just about every orchard situation, some provision needs to be made to move the drip outlets to different areas of the trees' root zones to prevent a lopsided concentration of roots and the possibility of disease because of constant moisture.

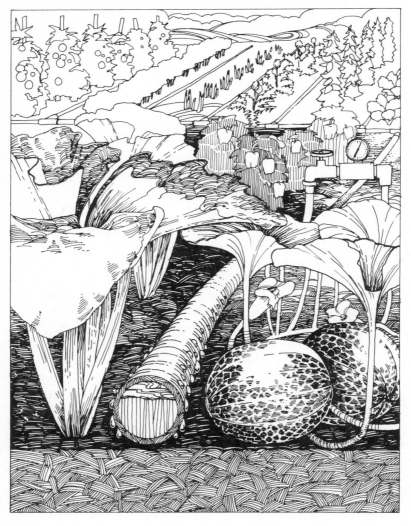

DRIP IrrIGATION SYSTEM

Water: Lifeblood of the Garden

You may also encounter the problem of too much flow at times. I found that where the ground isn't level there is a greater flow from the downhill emitters than the uphill ones as well as a tendency for greater outflow nearer the pressure tank than farther away from it. By experimenting with different diameter emitters and different size pipes, it's possible to get a more even flow, although I doubt it would make too much difference to the plants.

Positioning drip outlets for quick-maturing vegetables (radishes and seventy-day carrots, for instance) is too much hand labor for such a short period of time. Except for full-season vegetables, drip causes a lot of trouble during harvesting because you have to work around the lines.

The basic rule I follow, then, is to use drip for specific applications and in other situations, sprinkle.

There are dozen of different kinds of drip or trickle systems, some of them aboveground, some below. The one I'm most familiar with worked off a main water line, which was connected to a homemade pressure tank via a valve. The pressure in the tank could be adjusted by opening or closing the valve. Although some lines work on very low pressure, the one I used had to have twenty pounds on it to get a relatively even flow throughout the system. It also needed a filter to remove impurities from the river water we used. (Even the slightest impurity would clog the system.)

From the pressure tank the water ran through the filter into the PVC main lines. Feeder lines branched off the main lines down the rows of fruit trees. At each tree we drilled some holes in the line and set in a metal eyelet called a grommet. We then shoved "spaghetti lines," which is very thin tubing, into the grommets. To keep the spaghetti from pulling out, we took a piece of plastic pipe about two inches long, split it lengthwise, and slipped it over the pipe, grommet, and spaghetti. Another piece of split plastic pipe clamped the middle of

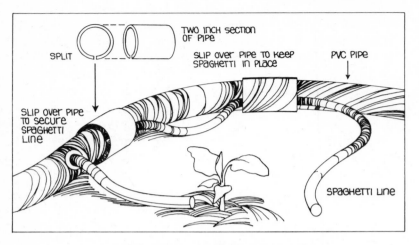

SECURING THE SPAGHETTI LINE

the spaghetti to the pipe, holding the spaghetti in the right place in relation to the plant.

(If this is too complicated for you because you're a gardener with only a backyard plot, simply skip the pressure tank and hook your system into an available city water supply, adjusting the pressure by opening or closing the spigot valve.)

The one method of watering I don't recommend is a hand-held sprinker. I have yet to meet the gardener who has the patience to stand in one spot and water an area long enough to give it the kind of soaking it needs. When I was a teen-ager I use to sprinkle daily because I thought that's what my vegetables needed. After all, they wilted by mid-afternoon. Eventually I figured out I was only watering the top inch or two of soil. Consequently the plants were becoming shallow-rooted. Between evaporation and transpiration the water quickly disappeared on hot days and my plants were barely able to survive. As soon as they used up the surface water they began to wilt because they had no root system in the deep, mineral-rich lower portions of the soil. Of course, I didn't water deep enough so that there would be a large reserve of

Water: Lifeblood of the Garden

water in the mid and lower reaches of the root zone by midsummer, anyway. I had created my own vicious circle that made me a slave to watering and my vegetables the victims of poor nutrition. In the many years since, I've seen scores of people repeat the same mistake. But it's one you can simply avoid—by careful and controlled irrigation in your own garden.

2
Practical Ways to Healthy Soil

Plants won't grow without food. That seems like an obvious principle, but when you read the history of formerly highly productive areas, or for that matter see some of the run-down and abandoned farms in this country, you realize a lot of farmers never got the message. They cleared the land and began farming with no thought of feeding. After a time production dropped off until the ground would barely grow a weed; then it was time to move on. A great portion of what is now desert in North Africa was incredibly productive wheat land that the Romans farmed for several hundred years to feed their legions until the land literally died. Today, most farmers rely on chemical materials to bolster the humus and nutrient-depleted land in much of this country. It's sad to realize that if it weren't for the use of these chemicals, we'd see some extraordinary deserts here, too.

In any garden or farm you can only expect optimum productivity if you take care to feed your crops and enrich the soil. All plants need hydrogen, carbon, and oxygen, which come from the atmosphere or water. They need the macronutrients nitrogen, phosphorus, and potassium, referred to in chemical and organic fertilizers as N, P, K, respectively. (Gardeners usually quote these three in numbers representing the percentage of each in the weight of a given quantity of fertilizer. Thus a fish emulsion with an NPK analysis of 5-2-2 contains five parts of nitrogen and two parts each of phosphorus and potassium, plus trace minerals.) Plants also need calcium and magnesium, which are both fertilizers and soil amendments (I'll talk more about them later), and the trace minerals or micronutrients.

In a nurserymen's training session I attended some

years ago in Hawaii, the instructor listed the trace elements—sulfur, boron, manganese, iron, molybdenum, copper, zinc, sodium, and chlorine—and said most were needed in only minute amounts. "A crop of carrots," he told us, "that yields 30,000 pounds to the acre might require 130 pounds of nitrogen, 30 pounds of phosphorus, and 190 pounds of potassium. In contrast it needs only a fraction of an ounce of molybdenum."

Some student would then always ask, "Then we don't have to worry about the micronutrients because the plants don't use much, right?"

The instructor quickly pointed out that that was entirely wrong. If that minute quantity of molybdenum is missing the plant will die as surely as if it were missing 190 pounds of potassium. Though plants use less of the micronutrients, their percentage in the soil is also correspondingly lower in terms of availability. The instructor cited as an example the pineapple industry in Hawaii, which almost collapsed in the early days because plants started showing severe disorders that normal NPK applications didn't cure. Finally someone discovered they needed small quantities of zinc and other trace elements, all of which were rapidly disappearing from the soil because the growers didn't know they needed to be replaced, or even that plants needed them.

In contrast, when I first became an organic gardener, I had a problem with overusing an element. I used much too much nitrogen because I had the philosophy that if a little bit is a good thing, a lot must be a great thing.

Tomatoes were my hapless victims. I set each transplant in a hole with about a gallon's worth of compost around the root system. I now know that this would have been an adequate starter, but to be sure I added a cup of bloodmeal just below the surface. About a month later I repeated the bloodmeal application. My tomatoes looked like a jungle by midsummer—the greenest, densest, lushest foliage you ever saw. Only one problem—there were no tomatoes.

I wondered what had happened. Did I need blossom-set hormones to keep the blossoms from falling off? No, there were hardly any blossoms at all. Did I fertilize enough? Yes, the plants seemed to be doing well. What then?

About that time a neighbor came by and happened to see my situation. "I see you've got leaf-itis," she said.

"What's that?"

"All leaves and no fruit," she explained. "That's what happened to me a couple years ago. My vines were beautiful, but no tomatoes. Too much nitrogen. What did you use?"

"Compost and bloodmeal."

"Right. Lots of bloodmeal, I bet. That's what I used. It's real concentrated nitrogen. If you use too much the plants will grow but they won't set fruit because of the imbalance. Less nitrogen, more phosphorus—that's the answer."

Since that rude awakening I've tried to balance my applications so that now through observation and referral to nutrient uptake charts I've determined how much of what each of my crops will require, and I'm confident that my soil, organically built up, contains enough of everything (and not too much of anything) for optimum growth.

For the gardener starting out, I recommend a soil test done by a professional laboratory as the first step, and I believe a periodic retesting (but certainly not in less than five years) is a wise procedure. A soil analysis will tell you the type of soil you have, its organic content, its acidity, nutrient content, and other pertinent facts, as well as give you suggestions for improvement. Your soil will lose nutrients through crop removal, erosion of wind and water, leaching, and chemical change. You must apply at least as much as the annual loss to maintain fertility. Mere chemicals won't do the job because they don't replace humus, and humus creates the environment for healthy growth.

For further discussion of the macro- and micronutrients, their effects, overabundances, and deficiencies, I suggest Gene Logsdon's *The Gardener's Guide to Better Soil*, and the United States Department of Agriculture's Yearbook for 1957, *Soils*, which offers informative material in relatively easily understood terms.

Humus For Healthy Growth

As I said, humus, that rich, black material, is the organic part of the soil that gives plants a healthy environment to live in. Lack of it is why some land that was highly profitable fifty years ago is wasteland today—despite the availability of chemicals. Whether it comes from compost, manure, or decaying animal and vegetable remains, humus contains nutrients that slowly become available to plants as microorganisms release them into soil where roots can pick them up. This is in direct contrast to the "shot in the arm" approach of chemical fertilization.

Humus improves soil structure remarkably, increasing both its breathing capacity (remember that plant roots absorb oxygen and carbon), and water-holding ability, while promoting large soil-animal populations from worms and moles down to the tiniest microbes—all of which contribute their lives to building up the soil. Humus is the center of my fertilization program. In some of my raised beds I think the percentage of humus in the soil easily rises above 20, but for ordinary purposes 5 percent humus is good, and 10 percent is phenomenal.

Composts, manures, and most mulches are both humus builders and excellent sources of macro- and micronutrients, and therefore make excellent natural fertilizers. Properly used, according to the guidelines in this chapter and the specific recommendations in the

31

HUMUS PROMOTES SOIL POPULATIONS

various vegetable sections, they'll promote soils that will yield healthy foods indefinitely. This is without the pollution and harm to soil and plants that often accompanies chemical fertilization.

The Natural Fertilizers

By using animal and plant wastes and remains I find I don't need a wide spectrum of fertilizers. All I need is what you need—what's locally available or, as in the case of finely ground rock fertilizers, what's naturally available.

Manure is my favorite natural fertilizer. It stimulates the work of soil microbes that unlock plant food held in soil-borne mineral compounds. It adds nutrients and humus to the soil, aids composting operations, and in the green state provides heat for cold frames as it decomposes. Lastly, it improves the physical condition of heavy soils.

I like fresh manure the best because I can process it myself. Aged manure that's been left to leach in the rain, or manure that's been allowed to heat up intensely without direction, is not worth much beyond its humus content. In the first instance water removes the nutrients; in the second, nutrients vaporize into the atmosphere. If you have access to your own manure supply— horses, chickens, goats—make sure the pile is neither soaking wet nor too dry. In the first case it will putrify, and in the second, heat up too much. I've found it helpful to cover each day's load with something absorbent. I use sawdust, but a layer of dirt, peat moss, or even newspaper will do the job just as well. This helps preserve nutrients.

I rarely put manure directly on the garden. It's more valuable to me in the green state as an ingredient in composts. Raw or rotten manure that's placed directly in the garden should be covered immediately if possible to prevent nutrient escape.

The manure's value depends on what type of animal it comes from and whether it's been mixed with bedding or other materials. Stable manure, which consists of manure plus bedding, is generally the material to choose when large amounts of manure are recommended. Chicken manure is generally the highest in all levels of plant nutrients, sometimes up to four times as rich as cow manure, but it contains far less humus. Horse manure is a little higher in most nutrients than cow and has the advantage along with chicken and sheep of being "hotter," that is, it decomposes faster and generates a higher composting temperature. Cow and hog manures are "cool." They're wetter and don't have as much nitrogen.

With stable manure as a guide, figure on placing 100 pounds of manure every 100 square feet. This is roughly twenty tons to the acre. I've never had more manure than I could use, so I tend to be very careful about where I put it. Composting it for specific purposes suits my needs. For example, by combining high nitrogen-content plants like stinging nettle and grass clippings with chicken manure it's possible to shape a compost ideally suited for gross feeders like cabbage. These special composts never burn the way fresh manures and chemicals can, and because of their nearly neutral state they don't promote harmful deposits of production-robbing acids.

There are still other natural materials that I use in my fertilization program. For instance, I use rock phosphate on a regular basis. Plant roots, microbes, and chemical actions in the soil combine to slowly release phosphorus from the finely ground rock. An application of ten pounds per 100 square feet of garden every five years, in conjunction with the amount you use in composts, the amount that falls on your land from the atmosphere, and the amount in manures and mulches should be more than adequate to meet most garden needs. I also sometimes use bone meal. It works faster but is much more expensive than rock phosphate and is best used in potting mixtures for indoor plants.

I happen to live in an area where potassium is in rather abundant supply, so I've never had to resort to potassium minerals like greensand and granite dust, but from what I understand the rate of application of these two naturally occurring potash sources are the same as for rock phosphate. (With potash making up approximately 5 percent of the dry rate of seaweed I figure I place more of this nutrient on my crops every year from this one source than my plants use in that season.) I do use wood ashes, both as a part of my composting operations and as a maggot killer around cole crops and as a slug barrier. They are an excellent source of potassium

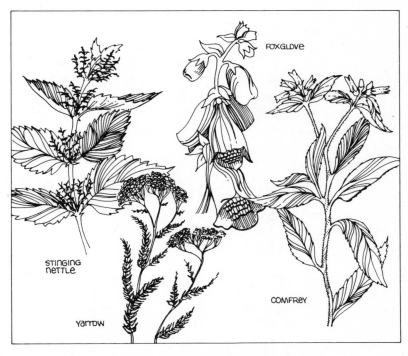

FOXGLOVE

STINGING
NETTLE

COMFREY

YARROW

WILD PLANTS USED FOR FERTILIZERS,

and some trace elements. Other sources of potassium include seaweed and manures.

Perhaps one of the most valuable sources of fertilizers that I know is weeds. Some of them concentrate certain elements in high quantities. I've pointed out that stinging nettle is high in nitrogen. I eat it and I compost it, and if it didn't grow wild abundantly where I lived, I would plant it. Some of the other wild plants that I use for fertilizer that appear to selectively accumulate elements are foxglove (gathers iron and manganese) and yarrow (collects potassium and calcium). I throw every kind of weed I can find into the compost except those from along roadsides that have been sprayed with chemicals as a control measure. Some other weeds like comfrey mine the subsoil for nutrients that would otherwise be unavailable to vegetables. I plant them along fencerows and utility poles for compost and chicken feed.

Lastly, there are a few other products that I find invaluable as fertilizers. Bloodmeal is one. It has a high (up to 15 percent) nitrogen content, and fair amounts of other necessary nutrients in a soluble form that makes it useful to growing crops or to stimulate bacterial action in compost piles. Sometimes I use shrimp meal to enrich calcium-loving crops like beets. I should also mention sewage sludge. It's available at times from municipal treatment plants as air-dried, digested sludge. But there's no way around it—it smells. If you work it into the ground immediately before planting a cover crop, and then follow with an aboveground crop, it should compare favorably with the average stable manure and not cause any sanitation objections.

Using Fertilizers
For an Extra Boost

So far I've talked about spreading these manures directly on the ground and working them into the soil.

ways to apply fertilizer

BAND APPLICATION: COMPOST AND DIRT ARE
USED TO FILL A FURROW, THE SEEDS ARE
PLANTED, AND THEN COVERED

SIDE-DRESSING: BLOODMEAL AND COMPOST
ARE PUT INTO A FURROW TO THE SIDE OF
THE PLANT

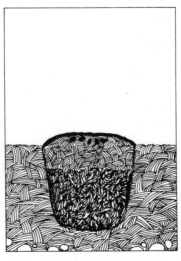

HILL APPLICATION: ONE TO SEVERAL
SHOVELSFUL OF COMPOST ARE MIXED
INTO A HOLE AND THEN THE SEEDS ARE
PLANTED

This is called broadcast application, and raises the general fertility of the land. It's an excellent way to stimulate microbial action and add humus, but some of the nutrients get lost to the plants because they change to an unavailable state, leach out of the soil, or the vegetable roots simply don't reach them. To offset this when fertilizer is scarce, or to achieve "booster" growth, many gardeners—myself included—sow the fertilizer in a narrow furrow or band either directly under or off to a side of the seed at planting time. This is called band application. I usually open a deep furrow, sprinkle in compost, spread dirt over that, sow seed, and cover. This is probably the most efficient method of applying fertilizer to one particular plant, but it doesn't provide for the overall enrichment of the land the way broadcast does. Thus it's a supplement and not a substitute.

A variation of the band application for use on widely spaced vegetables like squashes and melons is the hill application. This is nothing more than mixing one to several shovelsful of compost or rotted manure into a hole, covering with dirt, and planting the seed. Some folks remove all the dirt from holes a foot deep and as wide and replace with compost for crops like squashes, melons, and tomatoes.

Next there's the side-dressing. I use it for long-term vegetables and for those that respond to nitrogen for rapid, succulent growth. After the vegetables have shown some growth (details are in the chapters on specific vegetables), I apply bloodmeal, or a mixture of bloodmeal and compost four to five inches to the side of the plant in a furrow a couple inches deep. I cover and then water.

In some instances an even better method than side-dressing is the solution. For several years I've been using fish emulsions to fertilize transplants and plants already in rows. Manure tea, made by percolating water through a drum or barrel filled with manure or compost into a pail beneath, is a homemade variety of this principle. It has the advantage of allowing you to throw the spent manure into the compost heap where it will become humus.

There are three ways to use liquid fertilizers. One is to pour the fertilizer on the ground around the plant in lieu of watering. I do this quite often with tomatoes and cucurbits. A second way is to get a spray rig—hand or motorized—and spray the fertilizer on the leaves of plants. The third way is to attach a sprayer to your water hose and fertilize and water at the same time. Sprayers are inexpensive at garden centers. The plants will absorb the nutrients quickly. This is absolutely the fastest way I know to give ailing plants a vigorous boost, as well as an efficient way to correct deficiencies when they show up.

pH

While not specifically a fertilizer, pH, which is simply a measure of the relative acidity and alkalinity of the soil, and the soil amendments that alter pH, are inseparable from any fertilizer program.*

I learned my enduring lesson on this subject a couple of years after moving to northern California. In the heart of the Douglas fir and redwood region the pH is 5.5 or less. The soil in my garden was mostly clay. I limed it to lower the acidity of the soil and most crops grew well—except for beets. Each season my beets turned out small and woody. Then a friend told me to add additional lime to the beet furrow just before planting the crop. I did this and the results were a 100 percent improvement over the previous crop. Then I doubled the total application to most of the garden and continued to put dolomite in the beet furrows. The results were

---

*The pH scale runs from 1 to 14 with 1 measuring extreme acidity and 14 measuring extreme alkalinity. Seven is neutral.

even better. The lime not only assisted the beets, but it also improved the yields of other vegetables like broccoli and cauliflower. This intrigued me so I began to study pH and what it means to vegetables.

I found out that most crops thrive in the 6 to 7.5 pH range or, in other words, in slightly acidic or neutral soil. Some garden fruits, like blackberries and gooseberries, prefer a moderately acid soil, and a few thrive in strongly acid soil—for example, blueberries. I never add lime to such crops. A few other crops like potatoes and sweet potatoes like a moderately acid soil. The question, then, is how do we control pH? Except for those few crops that really require low pH (the main reason potatoes do, for example, is that below pH 5.5, the scab organisms that devastate crops can't live), the best course is to treat them all the same way, and that means keeping the soil in a slightly acid condition. This can be done in two ways: by adding organic matter or dolomite limestone.

Any organic matter you put in the soil will be slightly acidic in reaction. This means that if you have a soil on the alkaline side all you have to do is add humus-building composts, mulches, and green manures and over a period of time it will move toward a slightly acid condition. Peat moss, with a pH 4, is probably the quickest organic soil amendment you can use to bring down pH. If your soil is acid, the addition of organic matter will change the structure and raise the pH some unless it's already just slightly acid, in which case it will remain the same. Again, organic matter in large amounts tends to maintain any soil in a slightly acid condition.

Sometimes it's not possible to get the right pH by the addition of organic matter alone. In such cases I use agricultural dolomite. It's simply ground-up calcium carbonate and magnesium carbonate—natural limestone. Besides having the effect of raising the pH of the soil and making some chemically tied-up nutrients available for plant use, dolomite provides the necessary macronutrients calcium and magnesium.

As far as specific recommendations for liming go, I believe that any soil that remains at least pH 6 year after year, and which receives liberal applications of manures and composts, does not need lime. There are plenty of natural fertilizers which will help maintain a nearly neutral soil. For example, bone meal is pH 10, wood ashes 9 to 10, manures 8, and most city (not rain) water 9 to 10. If the soil shows magnesium deficiency at any point it might be wise to apply a small amount of lime, say two pounds per 100 square feet, every few years on clay or silt soils.

Where the pH is below 6 I suggest a total program of mulching, green manuring, manuring, and composting in addition to however much dolomite it takes to raise the soil to at least 6. In a heavy clay soil at 5.5 this could be about a ton to the acre, or about five pounds per 100 square feet. In a sandy soil half the amount would be used. Some people prefer to put twice as much on, and repeat the applications every three to five years, depending on production and rainfall (the more of either the faster the lime goes.) In my own garden I started with a fairly high initial application and now add small quantities (about one-fourth of the initial application) every year to maintain the pH in those sections of the garden that like a slightly acid soil. It's important to keep this concept of maintenance in mind when planning your liming program in relation to what I say about lime in each chapter. My recommendations are based on a continuously maintained garden, not a one-shot attempt.

Cover Cropping and Green Manuring

Closely tied in with both fertilization and pH are two important aids to optimum productivity—cover cropping and green manuring. Both subjects are well treated in Rodale's *How to Grow Vegetables and Fruits by the Organic Method* and Gene Logsden's *Gardener's Guide to Better Soils.* I'd like to add a few personal observations.

The objective of green manuring is to add humus to the soil. When nitrogen-fixing crops like clover and alfalfa, or deep subsoilers like comfrey are used as green manures it also means either the addition of nitrogen (from the legumes) or minerals (brought up by deep-rooted plants) to the vegetable-growing zone. Cover crops hold the soil in place when there's no vegetable crop growing as well as prevent nutrients from leaching. In the extremely winter-rainy north California coast where I garden, if I let the land lie uncovered for the entire winter the rains would erode the soil and water would percolate into the subsoil taking water-soluble plant nutrients from the vegetable root zone. A cover crop growing in winter prevents erosion and picks up and stores nutrients through the needs of its own life processes.

Cover crops are also energy-efficient. When you realize 95 percent of the bulk of a plant comes from water and the action of photosynthesis and only 5 percent comes from the soil, it's clear that growing something—even weeds—will harness the sun's energy and aid in the building of the biosphere. Covers also provide material for compost. Often I cut off all the cover at the soil level, allow the roots to decompose in the ground, and compost the tops. And when you have a severe weed problem a vigorous cover can outgrow and choke them out.

With green manuring and cover cropping the selection of the crop to be grown and its timing are of the utmost importance. I live in a rather moist, cool climate where frosts occur in the winter but where there's rarely a freeze. Crimson clover and purple vetch grow very well, but take some time to get established, so when I want to give a piece of land a rest from cultivation I sow a mixture of these two legumes in the fall after harvesting whatever crop was growing there. I allow the cover crop to grow the entire next year. Early the second spring I turn it under and a month to six weeks later plant a crop that thrives on nitrogen-rich soil. I give each portion of my garden this kind of treatment every five to seven years.

Under ordinary conditions I plant fast-growing annuals like rye or rape. A fall planting will result in a dense stand by the next spring which I then turn under. Where it grows well, and that seems to be any climate that's not naturally dry, buckwheat is a great choice, as its extensive root system helps break up hard soil.

If you are starting with rather poor soil you could build it up with a green manure program in the following way: In late spring, before they go to seed, turn under the initial weeds. In all green manure operations it's imperative that you cover whatever is growing with soil so rapid microbial activity can begin in a moist soil environment. Don't leave a stubby field. In about two weeks work up a coarse seedbed and sow buckwheat, and when it's eight inches high turn it under, wait another ten days, and sow again. Do this as many times as your growing season permits, allowing enough time to let the last crop be underground at least ten days before planting rye in early October (along the Pacific coast). The rye will grow all winter. Elsewhere it will make a start before the heavy frosts and snow and then take advantage of every warm spell. The following spring when the rye is nine inches high, turn it under, wait a couple weeks for it to decompose, and with the addition of organic fertilizers and soil amendments, your soil should be in good shape for almost any crop. Besides adding all that humus to the soil, green manures provide food for the bacteria that help build soil. Also where there is an abundance of humus the beneficial fungi that transfer nutrients directly into the root cells that they interpenetrate have a vigorous life. If it turns out after a year of green manuring that the plot is still in poor

A COVer CrOP ROTaTiON

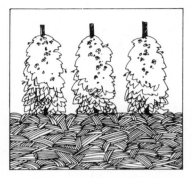

COLe CrOP IS PLaNTeD IN eaRLY SPRING

RuNNer BeaNS aRe PLaNTeD TeN DaYS aFTer COLe CrOP IS HarveSTeD

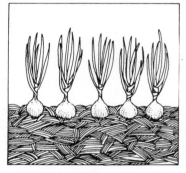

BeaNS aRe TuRNeD OveR WHeN THeY FLOWer

OverwiNTer WiTH ONiONS

condition (if, for example, you had subsoil that was leftover from a builder's bulldozing excavations) you can always repeat the cycle, or try a legume that will stand poor soils. Long-time local farmers and the county agricultural extension agents have been very helpful in telling me which green manures to grow.

The choice with cover crops is somewhat different. Peas are good for cool weather; try scarlet runner beans when it's a bit warmer. They produce a lot of green matter, and the nitrogen-fixing bacteria in their root nodules add fertilizer to the soil. In a typical plot I might set out nitrogen-using cole crops in the early spring, and about ten days after I harvest them (a little longer if the weather is unusually cold or dry) prepare the ground and plant runner beans. In early September the runners should be flowering nicely. I turn them under, wait another ten days, and sow an overwinter vegetable like onions or garlic. You'll note the sequence: aboveground vegetable that removes nitrogen; cover crop that returns humus and nitrogen to the soil when it otherwise would be idle; root crop that likes a loose, "humusy" soil and is able to grow during the winter.

There are endless variations on this basic principle, all geared to the amount of time you have to work with between crops and the result you desire. Green manuring and cover crops are the least expensive, least work-consuming ways I know to build up and help maintain the quality of your soil. They're also a good way to provide compost materials. They closely follow nature's principle of not leaving the earth bare, and are adaptable to every garden no matter how small.

3
Compost Is a Verb

As a young gardener I never knew about compost. In fact, compost wasn't just unpopular when I was growing up, it was practically unheard of. Around our house we bundled up all the kitchen scraps, leaves, and grass clippings and sent them to the garbage dump; then we bought packages of various kinds of chemical plant foods to improve our lawn and garden.

It wasn't until I spent a summer working for the University of Hawaii grounds department that I realized our mistake. Among my jobs there was sweeping the parking lots, which meant a pickup truck full of dusty debris, and accumulating large piles of grass clippings from an amphitheatre where it was growing particularly well.

Then the foreman devised a new task to keep me busy. First I passed all the debris I had collected through a quarter-inch mesh, eliminating the bottle caps, cigarette packages, and rocks. After that, I laid down a bed of grass clippings and leaves, spread dirt over the top of this layer, sprinkled some manure over that, and wetted it all down. I repeated the process until eventually I had to push a wheelbarrow up a ramp to get to the top of the heap. When it was done several weeks later it looked liked a mud-covered haystack. The foreman told me that all the junk would turn into beautiful black soil—just perfect for nursery potting mixtures. I recall being very skeptical, but several months later the refuse pile had indeed become rich, black plant food.

I forgot about that experience for several years until I was looking for alternatives to conventional farming practices. A friend recommended the book, *An Agricultural Testament*, by Sir Albert Howard. There in clearest detail was the Indore composting method—in essence the same one I had learned from the grounds department foreman. I suggest that you read that book, because you'll most likely never want to be without compost as long as you grow plants, whether you cultivate a thousand acres or grow a few flowers in pots on the window sill.

The Advantages of Composting

The beauty of composting is that it accomplishes so much. For instance:

It converts disease- and vermin-attracting garbage into a useful agricultural product at a considerable savings over conventional garbage disposal;

It promotes the efficient use of nutrients by plants by putting them into slow-release forms;

It takes the chemical energy of waste and transforms it into the useful energy of plant nutrients;

It increases the soil's water-holding capacity, and generally improves texture by adding humus. Humus, in turn, promotes a healthy microorganism life.

In short, composting is action. It's the action that reclaims or recycles organic and mineral materials for use in land fertilization or reclamation projects. Even that small compost pile I made for the grounds department fulfilled these criteria. A ton or so of useless dust that would have been washed out to sea by water or wind was reclaimed to grow useful plants. Grassy wastes, instead of being incinerated, were recycled for the same purpose. When you consider that everything that was ever alive can be recycled as compost, you can see that the problems of garbage, human waste, and refuse can be solved in a way that is not only ecologically more practical, but is also less expensive than any other method. Composting means the land benefits by a return of humus and nutrients; and it means we, in turn, will be healthier because our food will be grown naturally and the industrial processes used to make chemical fertilizers will be eliminated.

The Way to High Quality Compost

Over the years I've experimented with several methods of composting, all of them modifications of Sir Albert's basic process. At first I placed the materials in an enclosure made with chicken wire, a way that should satisfy most gardeners who don't make more than a ton or two at a time. Later I used an elaborate bin system, a method that's particularly good for people with somewhat larger gardens and more organic matter.

A friend built two bins for me that were side by side and share a common middle partition. The bottoms were made of heavy mesh six inches off the ground so air could reach the pile from underneath. Next to the bins was an inclined walkway and a platform to wheelbarrow

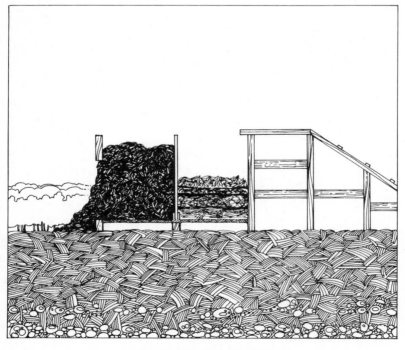

BIN SYSTEM FOR COMPOST

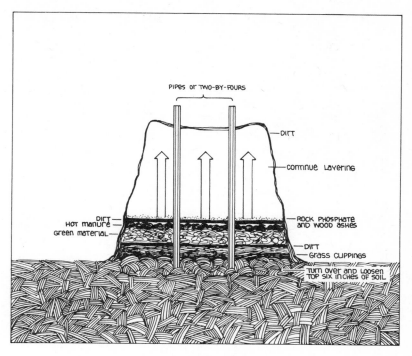

PIPES or TWO-BY-FOURS

DIrt

continue Layering

DIrt
HOT manure
Green material

ROCK PHOSPHATE
and WOOD ashes

DIrt
Grass CLIPPInGs

Turn over and Loosen
TOP SIX INCHes of SOIL

THE COMPOST PILE

materials to the top of the pile. I filled one bin the way I had at the University of Hawaii, adding two-by-fours or pipes vertically in the pile for aeration.

After three weeks or a month I removed the partition and took the compost from one bin and placed it in the other before replacing the partition. Then I filled the first bin again while the compost in the second completed breaking down. The outside wall of the second bin slid out so that I could remove the finished compost at ground level. If it wasn't quite ready it didn't matter. I spread it on the ground I was about to plow and it completed its breakdown in the soil just as it would in nature's garden. I was then ready to repeat the process, always having one pile starting and one finishing. During the winter months I placed heavy black plastic covers over the bins in order to prevent leaching and waterlogging.

The method I now use reflects the fact that I'm gardening in acres rather than in a couple hundred square feet, but the principles behind it are valid for every kind of aerobic composting, even on as small a scale as a garbage can with holes punched in the bottom. (Although certain ingredients would have to be adjusted if you were going to compost in that small a container to insure the correct carbon/nitrogen ratio.)

Below is my basic recipe for high quality compost. It took me several years of study and experimentation to arrive at this basic scheme, which I believe incorporates the best of several methods. The dimensions are for heaps six feet wide by five feet long by five feet high. This pile seems to be the smallest efficient size for unenclosed compost because it is just big enough to contain and hold heat. (The pile will heat up to 140° in a first stage, and then peak at 160°.) It also fulfills all the requirements for optimum performance: it will conserve nutrients, it won't heat up too much (overheating destroys microorganisms), and it will decompose in a reasonable length of time. The steps to follow, then, are these:

1. Turn over the top six inches of soil and loosen it. This is so soil organisms that assist in decomposition and in combining nutrients for later use by plants can come into the pile and multiply.

2. Set pipes or two-by-fours every two feet by two feet vertically in the pile, packing the ingredients up around them. When the desired height is reached, and just before sealing, pull them out. This leaves columns for air to circulate in the pile for quicker decomposition.

3. Next, put on a "heat blanket," which is simply a layer of grass clippings six inches deep. This layer next to the soil acts as insulation, a heat

source, and a moisture and nutrient absorber.

4. On top of the heat blanket place a thin layer of dirt, hardly more than half an inch.

5. Add a six-inch layer of green material from plants, shredded if possible. The material should be moist and well packed but not sodden.

6. On top of the vegetation place the hottest manure available. If it's fresh chicken manure spread an inch. If it's cow manure use two inches or three if it's mixed with a lot of bedding.

7. Put on a one-inch layer of dirt. If you have heavy clay soil in your garden, it's nice to use a sandy soil in this layer if available, and vice versa, to improve the texture of your garden dirt.

8. Sprinkle a pound of rock phosphate and a half-pound of wood ashes to twenty-five square feet. If you have an acid soil, also add a half-pound of dolomite.

9. Repeat the sequence, sloping the pile slightly inward so it will hold together better. When it's five feet high make a slight depression in the center running nearly the full length to act as a basin for subsequent waterings.

10. Cover the entire heap with a layer of dirt. This is very important since the compost should never be left uncovered in the initial heating process. If it is, heat, moisture, and nutrients in gaseous form will escape and the compost won't be of the best quality.

11. Turn the pile after six weeks. It's safe at this point to introduce earthworms into the outer edges. If you don't want to turn the pile you don't have to, but be ready for the decomposition to take many months or even years.

The result of all of this is a very rich, black, organic soil with all the elements necessary for plant growth and human nutrition. The final nutrient analysis will depend on the materials you started with and how carefully you kept them from leaching in water or through the atmosphere. I apply the finished product all over the garden to a depth of two or three inches and work it into the topsoil.

Books like Rodale Press's *Complete Book of Composting* (now out of print) will give you a good deal more information on the subject, but I do have to admit that I'm very partial to my plan. It covers all the important points of composting, and although it may sound a little mystifying and difficult on paper, it's really very simple in practice. In addition, it has the advantage of allowing you to tailor-make composts for specific plants by changing the amounts of various raw materials rich in specific elements. A compost made with all the green matter coming from grass clippings, for example, will be rich in nitrogen and good for salad greens. One made from seaweed will be a good source of potassium and just right for root crops.

But no matter what specific ingredients you use or how you construct your pile, remember, compost is a verb. You've got to do it.

4
To Mulch
or Not to Mulch

Two camps have arisen in the organic movement over the question of whether or not to mulch. There are those who keep their gardens under permanent mulch the year-around and those who continue to spade or plow their ground every year.

Ruth Stout popularized the first approach in her book, *How to Have a Green Thumb without an Aching Back*. Basically the method she describes tries to imitate nature. When left undisturbed, leaves and dying vegetation in the forests and grasslands form a mulch of organic matter that microorganisms digest into humus. Year after year, century after century, new seeds sprout and grow, more vegetation accumulates on the earth, and the soil gets richer and richer. In a similar way, the permanent mulcher places a thick covering of hay, grass, or other suitable material over the whole garden, only exposing the topsoil when planting seed. Theoretically the soil always remains friable because the mulch next to the soil is breaking down into nutrients and humus as more matter is put on top to maintain the depth of the mulch (usually six to eight inches).

The second camp continues to turn the ground over, and to perform other operations like cultivating and cover cropping along with mulching as part of an integrated gardening program. (It's interesting to note that nature periodically removes a portion of the mulch and undergrowth in the forest through fires started by lightning or other methods. Forestry experts are now seriously looking into the seed-sprouting and forest-renewal aspects of the controlled burn. This indicates to me that even nature takes a break from the permanent mulch.)

Naturally there are pros and cons for both methods. I sum up my position this way: Permanent-mulch gardens work and they don't require as much labor as other organic methods, but you won't get optimum production in a permanently mulched garden. Since my main emphasis is on optimum returns from soils in optimum condition, I use mulch in many ways for many purposes, but never on a permanent basis.

Using Mulch

Why is mulch such a handy thing to have around the garden? First of all, it acts as a buffer between the surface soil and the air, breaking up the pull of evaporation. Water stays in the ground instead of vaporizing into the atmosphere. That buffer effect also protects the soil from wind erosion. These two facts alone have convinced me to keep my garden covered all the time, either with a mulch, with growing plants, or with both. When a soil is covered, bacteria, fungi, microorganisms, enzymes, earthworms, insects, and small animals beneficial to soil and crop health have both a home and a food supply. They take the raw material of mulch, whether it's hay, seaweed, straw, sawdust, shredded newspapers, or any one of a dozen other materials, and help turn it into nutritious soil that vegetables thrive in.

In the summer mulch keeps temperatures down around plants. This helps them cut down on water loss through transpiration and also keeps them from the stresses associated with temperature extremes. In some instances I've noticed a dramatic difference between mulched and unmulched rows. I could comfortably walk through a cabbage patch mulched with grass clipping— in my bare feet at midday—one summer. A few yards away in the same garden bare ground was being prepared for a late broccoli crop. The ground there was so hot it burned my feet. That coolness also allowed me to have a decently flavored cabbage past the time cabbages usually get bitter.

In that same garden I had a severe pigweed and ragweed problem wherever I wasn't able to get sufficient mulch to adequately cover the ground. Where the ground was covered, as among the cabbages and broccoli, there was no weed problem. Deep mulch always stops most weed growth. When weeds do come up they are spindly and easily controlled by hand.

When the crop is gone, and you're not going to immediately plant another, mulch continues to protect your soil. It breaks up rainwater so that it filters down into the soil rather than slams against it, washing away topsoil and leaving a crusty surface. Finally, where winters are severe enough to cause heavy frost, the mulch will act as a heat barrier to protect biennials and perennials from changes in the weather.

Kale, Squash, and Mulch

To give you an idea of how I mulch I'll take two crops, the cool weather-loving kale and the hot weather-loving winter squash and explain how I deal with both.

Kale does not like heat. The leaves get tough, and its taste gets offensive. In hot summer areas it must be kept cool for good results. As soon as possible after the main heavy winter rains are over I prepare the ground. Stirring up the soil helps me get some of the nutrients that have leached down up to the top as well as helping to move materials that have been acted on beneficially by weather and microorganisms incorporated into the soil where roots will be able to pick up their nutrient load (remember wind, water, and temperature are partners with animals in nature's soil-building process). I also warm up the soil by spading or plowing since there is no way you can warm it up with a permanent mulch. You have to wait until the sun heats up that thick cover and

HOW TO MULCH KALE

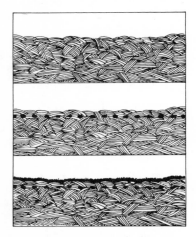

AFTER THE GROUND IS STIRRED UP AND THE SEEDS ARE PLANTED, APPLY A SAWDUST MULCH

APPLY SEAWEED SIX INCHES DEEP AROUND GROWING PLANTS

AFTER PLANTS ARE HARVESTED, TURN UNDER MULCH FOR SHEET COMPOST

then heats the soil.

With my soil warm and uncovered I plant the kale and cover the whole plot with a very light—not more than a half-inch—layer of well-rotted sawdust. I use

56

sawdust early in the spring because it's easy to apply in a thin layer, and the rotted material is almost black and therefore a good heat absorber. I only use enough to protect the topsoil from the elements because I want to continue to encourage the heating of the soil.

Once the kale is growing vigorously and the hot weather is beginning, I apply a seaweed mulch six inches deep. In the early spring the kale needed all the heat it could get for quick growth, but as the season advances there is ample heat, which now needs to be controlled for the benefit of the plant. My seaweed mulch does this. It keeps the crop cooler in the daytime, while conserving ground heat during the night like a blanket. This gives the plants a more even growing temperature, which is particularly important where day-night temperatures are extremes such as in deserts, mountains, or northern areas. Also, as the seaweed decomposes, it releases a host of macro- and micronutrients, humus, amino acids, hormones that stimulate plant growth, and simple sugars that helpful bacteria thrive on. Besides all that the seaweed (or any mulch) looks nice. It gives the garden a sense of cleanliness and order.

I maintain the mulch as long as the kale is growing, adding more if any bare spots or weeds appear. With kale and most other vegetables I draw the mulch right up and around the plants like a scarf. When the crop is fully harvested, I either let the mulch remain as a cover until I'm ready for some new gardening operation, or I turn it under, remake a seedbed, and plant a new crop. My former mulch now performs like a sheet compost, which, by the way, is nothing more than taking compostable materials in their raw or semidecayed form and turning them under to complete decomposition.

Squashes will barely grow under the weather conditions in which kale achieves its best growth, so I handle mulching in a different way. Kale will germinate in 40° weather; squashes want 60°. I've successfully started them outdoors in hills as early as mid-April by working whatever mulch was on the ground in the early spring into the soil. Since a high organic matter content produces a looser soil that warms up faster, mulch serves a valuable purpose even when it's turned under. I leave

HOW TO MULCH SQUASH

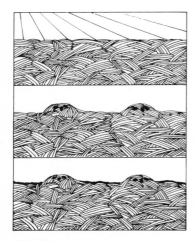

AFTER OLD MULCH IS TURNED UNDER, PLANT SEEDS IN HILLS AND LAY MULCH EVERYWHERE EXCEPT ON THE HILLS

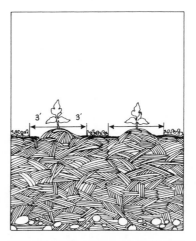

WHEN THE PLANTS START TO RUN, MULCH EVERYWHERE EXCEPT IN A CIRCLE THREE FEET IN DIAMETER FROM THE CENTER OF THE HILL

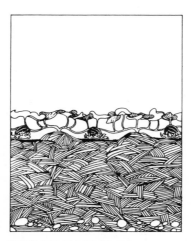

SQUASH RESTS ON A BED OF MULCH

the ground bare for about a month to warm up and for the mulch to decompose.

Then I plant, and as with kale, I lay down a light mulch all over the patch except on the hill where I plant the squash. Once the plants start to run I lay down a thick mulch everywhere except in a circle three feet in diameter from the center of the hill. Sun rays are able to hit the earth directly and warm up the soil until the squash forms its own living mulch. One extra benefit with a mulch for squashes and for all vine crops like watermelons or unstaked tomatoes is that the fruit rests on a light, airy bed relatively free of the decomposition activity of soil organisms. This means cleaner fruit and less spoilage. Mulch also protects the soil from compaction by your feet or machinery if you plant in rows. With vine crops like squash I like to use hay or straw because they make a lighter bed than seaweed or leaves.

Mulch Is Everywhere

One thing that I want to make clear is that I don't favor one material over another across the board for mulching, although I do favor some for certain purposes. First I see what's locally available. In my case that means sawdust from California's redwood and fir mills, seaweed from the ocean, leaves from the forest, and hay and straw when I can get them. In other places I've used grass clippings which have the added advantage of being an excellent source of nitrogen. I almost always end up using newspapers for one purpose or another, and burlap is quite useful as a mulch for seeds starting in flats. I've heard of folks using ground corncobs, peat moss, coconut fiber, various kinds of hulls, worn-out clothing, wood chips, rotted wooden boards, and just about everything else that will biodegrade in a clean, safe manner.

Sometimes I even use inorganic mulches like stones. If you've ever lifted up a big rock in a dry field you've probably noticed it was moist, there was evidence of worm and insect activity, it seemed the grass growing right around the edge of the rock was faring better than that farther away in the field, and maybe you even found a newt or snake curled up under it. I sure have. You can do just about anything you do with other mulches with rocks. They even decompose and release nutrients into the soil at a slow rate. Because of their weight and general unwieldiness I think they do best around permanent crops like berry bushes or dwarf fruit trees. In the ornamental garden their effect can be very striking. If you have a lot of them put some in the garden instead of in the fencerow—maybe between the rhubarbs—as an experiment.

Another mulch that utilizes on-the-spot materials is the dust mulch. I suspect this method is as old as farming, and is widely practiced today where wheat growers allow thousands of acres to lie fallow in dry areas. The farmers plow their fields after a harvest in August and then disc them. Snow covers the fields in winter and in spring, when the ground is workable, the farmers disc again and again, working up a thick dust mulch. In late summer they plant. Meanwhile the dust acts as a buffer between the moisture-laden soil and the air because capillary evaporation is broken up by the loose, dry dust particles. And since weeds don't grow, there's no moisture loss. By the end of two winters there's enough soil moisture to mature the crop planted in autumn.

These same principles hold true in the garden. You can make dust mulch for any crop in a couple weeks by hoeing up the ground every couple of days until there's a loose layer two or three inches deep. The dust will be hot, but the ground underneath will be cooler than if there was no mulch, and you will conserve moisture and eliminate weeds. The drawback with this method, obviously, is that a lot of soil blows off the land as dust, and it would be much better to have an organic mulch over the ground. I can only see using a dust mulch in the extreme case of not having any other kind of mulch during a period where there was no water available. Such a situation isn't likely to happen in a small garden, though it could happen on an organic farm.

If you ever are in a no-mulch situation you might want to consider inorganic mulches like plastic, glass wool, or fiberglass before resorting to dust. I've never bought any of these products. They're energy-intensive, they don't add to the humus and mineral content of the soil, and some of them, like polyethylene, give off gasses that may be detrimental to living organisms. On the other hand, they are all unusually good conservers of moisture, they last for several seasons, and if you use black-colored materials, they warm up the soil more efficiently in early spring than any other kind of mulch I've heard of. I say use man-made materials if they're available free (as they often are around fruit-packing sheds) and you don't have access to enough organic mulches, or when you want to do some specialized garden work like heating up the soil for an early tomato planting.

No matter what materials you use, mulch everything in your garden, lightly with dark materials when temperatures are cool and you want to warm the soil, and heavily with whatever material is available when you want to moderate extremes. Everywhere you mulch you protect your soil, keep it relatively free from erosion, stimulate soil life, and develop a rich humus.

5
Pests, Diseases, and Weeds

When it comes to pests, diseases, and weeds, my experience has been that there are few problems in well-cared-for organic soil. Those problems that do occur probably indicate one of three things: You're not paying attention to some important cultural practice; the vegetable under attack is not suitable to the environment; or the soil is not very fertile or high in humus. It's impossible for me to give you a thorough treatment of each of these three major problem areas because they're each technical subjects that fill volumes by themselves, but I feel I can give you an overview so that you'll know how to approach problems if they do arise.

To start with, I learned early in my career that most of the successful gardeners I knew really knew very little about insects, diseases, or what weeds were in their garden. That's because their focus wasn't on the negative, but on the positive—how to make a garden so healthy that the problems didn't appear. They practice what I call a preventive approach to gardening.

But that's something very different from what chemical gardeners who routinely spray their crops with pesticides and disease-fighting medications call "prevention." They don't spray because there's a problem, they spray because they *might have* one. I don't call that prevention at all. I call that a pathological approach for it kills plants and animals of all classes, poisons food and the environment, and costs a lot of money. I've had to work with these chemicals when I was employed by nonorganic growers, and just the cautions on the labels were enough to make my hair stand on end. I've never seen any result from using chemicals except a growing dependence on them to control those factors that lessen or ruin crop production. In this chemical age even organic gardeners sometimes get tempted to buy a cheap bottle or can of some highly touted "safe" chemical cure for the bugs that are eating their tomatoes or cabbages. I caution you: Don't do it. Chemical controls are a Pandora's box that will give you more problems in the end than you had at the beginning. For an interesting treatment of the subject I recommend Sir Albert Howard's *The Soil and Health*, Rachel Carson's *Silent Spring*, and Beatrice Trum Hunter's *Gardening without Poisons*.

The Good Bugs vs. the Bad Bugs

The way I look at it we will have insects in the garden, but hopefully the good guys will offset the bad guys. I help to give good bugs the competitive edge in several ways. First, I make sure my soil is healthy and my agricultural practices sound. I build up the soil with humus and nutrients along the lines presented in this book, maintain the pH within the range vegetables thrive in, grow most plants in season (forced plants are more susceptible to disease), use varieties suited to the environment, and do my weeding on time. I also make sure plants receive proper sunlight and water, and are not crowded or competing with weeds.

Second, it's just as important to have a reasonable attitude toward insects in terms of the damage they actually cause. When I worked in commercial orchards I quickly found out that a significant portion of the price of an apple, pear, or cherry is in the sprays and cultural practices employed to make the fruit conform to U.S. Department of Agriculture "Extra Fancy" standards: standards which primarily define appearance rather than quality. I certainly believe we should strive for the best possible appearance and that, in fact, the "Extra Fancy" label is well within the range of normal organic practices. But what we need to do is disregard the unreasonable definitions of "quality"—the ones that say because there are a few earwigs in the large bottom leaves of a cabbage that the vegetable is not fit to eat or the garden is in-

GARDEN PESTS

fested. In truth a few blemishes on our apples or holes in the lettuce leaves will in no way affect quality. If you can learn to accept these and other indications of pest activity, many of your insect and microorganism problems will be over. Anyway, better the bug than a plant laced with methoxychlor, chlordane, or malathion.

Now in the event you do have a bonafide insect invasion on your hands, I recommend *Organic Plant Protection* edited by Roger B. Yepsen, Jr. as your sourcebook on controls. Other interesting information is found in the Brooklyn Botanical Garden's *Handbook on Biological Control of Plant Pests,* and Helen and John Philbrick's *The Bug Book.*

Fighting Disease

I've found Mr. Yepsen's book an invaluable source of information on diseases, too, though as with pests, a healthy soil and wise cultural practices will solve most problems, and toleration the bulk of the rest. There are some 50,000 plant diseases in the United States alone. It makes more sense to try not to have them than it does to learn what they are and how to cope with them. I've found that there are several specific things you can do to help minimize disease.

The right site does the most to prevent problems. Wet locations where drainage is poor will be a breeding ground for root diseases, mildew, and fungus pests. Shading heat-loving plants is another invitation to trouble, as is planting crops too close to trees where the latter exert a powerful pull on the available nutrient supply.

After the site is chosen, build the humus. Lack of humus inhibits the growth of a certain type of fungi that interpenetrates crop root hairs and provides them with soluble nutrients.

Next, use resistant varieties where disease is a special and continuous problem. Happily, I think the resistant genes that were bred out of popular vegetables through lopsided breeding programs and chemical farming techniques (to emphasize looks, huge production, and marketing qualities), are now being reintroduced.

Rotate your crops. This helps prevent soil-borne diseases from building up. Rotation also keeps certain plants that concentrate particular nutrients from mining the soil and thus bringing nutrient-deficiency diseases on themselves.

Keep your garden clean. When you find a diseased plant, remove it from the garden, being as careful as possible not to touch any other plant, and then try to identify the disease. Don't let just any old weed grow in the garden. Weeds often carry diseases and pests that affect cultivated plants. If you accidentally break a plant use a clean knife to cut off the damaged part. Thin out all scraggly and atypical plants. This process, called roguing, eliminates the weak ones where disease often gets a foothold.

Lastly, one of the greatest factors promoting disease in the organic garden is an imbalanced nutrient content—usually an excess of nitrogen. Beginning gardeners are most prone to this problem because it's so easy to dump a lot of bloodmeal, for example, on a patch of ground. Rarely do they put enough nitrogen on to cause the plant to show signs of poisoning, but enough that vegetables send out lush, sappy growth. This makes the plant abnormal, and it becomes the target of whatever disease organisms are in the environment. Moderate, uninterrupted growth in healthy soil is the best preventive against these nutrient problems and, I believe, the basis of a general vigor that wards off all other pest and disease problems.

Weeds: Eradication and Management

Weeds are not only linked with pests and diseases, but in my garden they're usually the greater problem. As

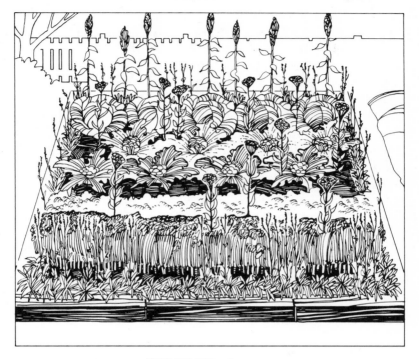

BeneFICIaL WeeDS

I pointed out, weeds harbor or transmit many garden problems. They must be controlled or they'll overrun you in a few weeks. On the other hand, control doesn't mean eradication.

My favorite definition of weeds is the one that says, "Weeds are plants growing where you don't want them." In the garden they may be pernicious troublemakers, but in another environment they may be just the thing to renew worn-out land. Or they may be medicinal plants or an important source of food for wild animals. This means I treat weeds in two ways, depending on the variety and circumstances: I either eradicate them or I learn to manage them.

In my first northern California garden thistles came up everywhere. They were small plants and I had no

67

trouble weeding them out. Unfortunately they not only grew in the garden but all around the garden as well. I quickly saw that if I didn't control those around the garden, just one plant going to seed would reinfest the whole area. At first I cut the brush, but the thistles easily came back. Then I cut them off at ground level, but that gave them just enough encouragement to come up with two or three stems instead of one. Finally I bought a pair of horsehide gloves and pulled them out by hand all summer and fall. This reduced my problem to occasional maintenance.

This may sound like a good deal of work, but another thistle story will illustrate the necessity of control with some of the more noxious weeds. Several years later I worked a new garden where thistles infested about 5,000 square feet of good land. The rotovator sliced the roots to pieces, only to have them promptly reroot and put out new growth—just about the time the peanuts and corn I had planted began to germinate. There were so many of them that I couldn't begin to pull them by hand. I had to be content, because the area was so large, to hoe them as deeply as possible. Throughout the season I had to hoe and hoe and hoe. Eventually the corn shaded the thistles and acted as a living control. The peanuts didn't fare as well, however. The thistles constantly returned and would have choked them out if given the opportunity. With weeds like thistles you absolutely have to eradicate them or they'll take over your garden and you'll spend a great deal of time just trying to save it. I spent as much time on those 5,000 square feet as I did on the rest of the two-acre garden, and I never did get the weeds completely under control that season. The lesson is that whatever the persistent weeds are in your garden, destroy them or they'll be a constant drain on your energy and productivity.

Besides running over a garden, weeds rob plants of moisture and nutrients, harbor noxious pests and diseases, and reduce crop yields. Generally speaking they have a take-over power that far outstrips most vegetables' ability to grow. A weed next to a vegetable will cut into the plant's nutrient supply, water supply, and if it's a tall grower, shade out the vegetable. The result is a reduced yield. There are also weeds that specifically harbor such pests as cabbage bugs, Japanese beetles, or squash bugs and act as alternate hosts for some diseases. (Clubroot in cabbages will persist in nearby wild mustard. Unless you eradicate the mustard from the garden you'll never control the clubroot in your cabbages.)

As I said, though, I am not a proponent of clean cultivation. My second way of handling weeds is management, a method which reflects the fact that in nature there are all kinds of plants growing in close proximity. Clean cultivation, the elimination of every plant except the crop you're growing, is contrary to nature. Diseases and pests can zero in on a single crop easily, but a profusion of plants, each with its own particular hormones, secretions, colors, and nectars, combine to confuse troublemakers or decoy them from the crop plants. It might take some getting used to to see a big pigweed towering up among the cabbages, or a few yarrow plants scattered down the rows, but I know from experience that it's possible to bridge the gap between clean cultivation and managed-weed gardening.

The biggest help to me in doing this was to view weeds as crops, green manures, or covers. For example, some weeds, like stinging nettle and sow thistles, are subsoilers and soil improvers. Yet others are nurse plants with root systems that go down deep into the soil and actually make a highway for vegetable roots to travel. Others are shademakers for small crops that like cool weather, and still others are living mulches or have food value. In my own garden there are several weeds that illustrate these uses. Yarrow, chickweed, the species of euphorbia called gopher plant, purslane, sheep sorrel, and nettle are among my favorites.

Yarrow seems to have a toning effect on nearby

plants. It tends to strengthen the aromatic qualities of herbs. I also use it as a home remedy for coughs, colds, and fevers. I allow it to remain everywhere it doesn't interfere with vegetable crops, like along fences and sheds. I also let it grow up here and there in the garden. If it takes up the space of one carrot, or reduces the yield of a broccoli plant by a mouthful, it probably encouraged the growth of six other carrots, or spurred some broccoli-loving bug to go elsewhere for a meal.

Chickweed is my favorite self-sowing living mulch. It's also an excellent medicine for skin problems. I often let the chickweed grow up where a mulch is old or thin. It grows all winter in mild areas and quickly makes a living mulch that can be harvested as a chicken feed or used as an addition to salads.

Gopher plants grow tall and wide in my garden, and I like to see one every thirty to forty feet. They secrete a substance in their roots that repels gophers, which is particularly helpful among the root crops. If you haven't experienced gopher problems, let me explain that these animals dig tunnels underground and when they get on a row of carrots, for example, they will first eat one root, then the next, and so on down the row. Sometimes they draw the whole plant into the burrow and eat the root and greens. Other times they leave an inch of root and the tops. You think you have a healthy crop until you pull the carrots and find a row of greens and stubs. Gopher plants break up this pattern, and if you have enough all around the garden, force the animals to look for more favorable pastures.

Sheep sorrel is just plain hard to get rid of. Half the time I battle to keep it out of the garden where its huge root and runner system interferes with and entangles itself in crops. The other half of the time I let it grow along borders for diversity and because I like to eat it.

I've mentioned nettle before in other contexts. Like the yarrow it has a good effect on other plants. It's also good for composts and to eat.

Purslane is a good example of a nurse plant and living mulch. Though it creeps along the ground it has a very deep taproot that acts as a channel for ordinarily shallower-rooted crops to follow. I let it grow mainly in pathways or in areas where I don't happen to have the time to plant something else immediately. Though I'm not particularly fond of it as a food, many people are. In Latin America it's commonly found in markets.

These are just a few of the hundreds of weeds that can play a valuable role in the garden. Properly managed, they contribute to the health and vigor of your vegetables, and the balance of the garden ecosystem. However, lest you think my garden is overrun with weeds, I want to repeat that I don't let just any weed grow. I'm continually aware of the state of growth and the relationship the weeds bear to other plants. I don't allow very many to live within the vegetables. It only takes one or two every ten or fifteen feet to give the mixture effect because I also grow flowers and herbs throughout the garden.

Whenever a new species of weed enters my garden I identify it and check through my books on companion planting and edible and medicinal plants to see if it has a special value to me or my vegetables. If it does, and it's not a robber of soil nutrients, a disease carrier, or extremely difficult to control, I find a niche for it in the total garden scheme. You can do the same in your garden. The county extension service will help you with identification and reference books will tell you the rest. Among the books I've found most valuable, either for identification or for determining the value of weeds are Jethro Kloss's *Back to Eden,* Joseph Meyer's *The Herbalist,* John Lust's *The Herb Book,* Oliver Medsger's *Edible Wild Plants,* and Donald Kirk's *Wild Edible Plants of the Western United States.* From a purely botanical point of view, *Gray's Manual of Botany* seems to be the best general reference on common wild plant identification for both native and introduced species.

71

PART II:
Getting Even More from the Garden

6
Planning Makes Perfect

An ancient proverb warns, "Without a vision the people perish." So it is with gardens. The key to success is in foresight and attention to details. Like a carpenter who has an architect's rendering and a set of house plans before he starts to build, when I construct my garden I start with a plan, move to a plot layout, and then continually revise it on the job as circumstances change or new ideas crop up.

My first consideration is last year's garden. I look at how well the different seeds I planted germinated and produced, and if it seems that despite my careful work the crop didn't meet my expectations, I discard that seed strain, or give it a second chance in a short row.

I also reevaluate my methods, trying to be as flexible as possible. For instance, I started with row cropping, had a brief infatuation with raised beds, and went back to rows. Now I've come to the conclusion that a combination of raised beds, rows, and ground-level beds is most suitable. Had I stuck to one way with a "this is the way I've always done it and this is the way I'm always going to do it" attitude I would have missed a valuable method of gardening. Thoughtful evaluation led me to try the raised beds. When I found them unsuitable I laid them aside, but I didn't close my mind to the concept entirely because I saw it had its good points. Eventually I figured out ways to make raised-bed planting worthwhile. The result: progressive changes in my gardening.

On the other hand, wholesale adoption of new or novel ideas is not good gardening. I know a man who got an idea to grow luffa gourds for the bath sponge trade. He took up some very good land and planted seed, disregarding the fact that the luffa is a hot weather-loving plant, and that he lived in a cool, foggy climate.

"How's it going?" I asked him in August.

"Wonderful," he replied, pointing to a profusion of vines and young fruit.

In November I saw that same fruit. Not a single one had matured, though all were full size. They were rotting on top of a compost heap, the victims of poor planning. The erstwhile entrepreneur had nothing but empty pockets to show for his plunge into the sponge business.

Tools to Use

When I've gone over the last year's garden I turn my attention to tools. I garden year around but the main work load is between early spring and mid-autumn. I find the end of the season the perfect time to repair and service equipment and buy new tools.

At the beginning of the season prices are often high and service hard to come by. Recently, when I borrowed the Lighthouse Ranch's new rototiller to work up a spring planting bed, I found the machine didn't work as well as it should have. I called the garden shop and the owner told me there were literally dozens of people with lawn mowers, tillers, edgers, and small garden tractors all clamoring to get their engines serviced immediately so they could begin the season. It looked like my operation was going to get set back a couple weeks, but as a special act of kindness the mechanic took some time off his backlog to check my engine. Had he not done that, a few adjustments could have cost me many days and dollars in down time. That same mechanic in November had hours on his hands to give me advice on which tiller to buy, how to operate our garden, the state of the nation, and the best way to file income tax.

As far as tools go, the size of the garden and the strength and/or time of the gardener are the primary factors in deciding what is needed. For years I used nothing more than a spade, a spading fork, one garden rake, one leaf rake, a mattock and grub hoe (better than

TOOLS TO USE IN THE GARDEN

shovels for breaking up hard ground and skimming tough weeds off the surface), a sledgehammer for driving stakes, a cane knife (similar to a machette) for cutting brush and things like cornstalks, a few small tools like trowels and water buckets, and a couple lengths of hose and nozzles. For the average garden this ought to suffice. When I got a bigger garden I found a rototiller with an engine mounted in front of the tines and with cultivating and shredding attachments was a great labor saver. (Before the tiller I worked nearly an acre by hand with help from my friends.)

For acreage I found a tractor and rotovator attachment were just the thing for tilling in spring. The rotovator does what a rototiller does, only quicker and deeper. In two sweeps at right angles to each other it's possible to work up a seedbed from unplowed ground. When I say tractor, I mean a real tractor, not one of those garden models. As far as I'm concerned a good heavy-duty rototiller will take you to the place where the smaller standard model tractors take over. In talking to many farmers I've found they generally dislike the garden models, not because they're not powerful enough for what they're designed to do, but because they don't hold up well mechanically. Besides, a full-size tractor can do all the same work more efficiently. I've seen good, used tractors for sale cheaper than you can buy a new and good quality rototiller.

The other two pieces of equipment I consider necessary for bigger gardens is the high-wheel cultivator with several different attachments and a seeder with different discs. Seeders are especially nice when other people help you plant. Last season I gave a young woman an ounce of onion seed and told her to sow a few rows in a short section of garden where I had run out of cauliflower. She came back a little later and said she had finished the job.

"Where did you put the leftover seed?" I asked.

"I planted it."

"Where?"

"Right where you told me."

Now I figured she should have used probably one-tenth of the amount of seed in that packet. Beginners almost invariably think they have to plant lots of seed. The result is waste and trouble thinning. Even a small, inexpensive seeder will pay for itself in a few seasons when you figure the time and seed saved in sowing as well as reduced thinning time.

There are also a few miscellaneous things that come in handy. The wheelbarrow and cart are two pieces of equipment that I find necessary for my work. Burlap sacks, string for laying out rows, tape measures, stakes and trellises, and flats are very useful. The standard flat sizes are twelve by eighteen inches and eighteen by eighteen inches by three inches deep. The end pieces should be of three-quarter-inch stock, the sides and bottoms of one-half-inch wood, and there should be half-inch holes in a five-spot arrangement drilled into the bottoms for drainage. But in a pinch anything will do for a flat. Last year I used some old dresser drawers.

Where to Plant What

Laying out the garden is best done on site with paper, pencil, and imagination. I divide my garden into sections based on a rotation program. There are also special sections set aside for perennials.

Early spring and late fall crops go in the warmest, most protected place, preferably one with a southern exposure. San Francisco is hardly the city you'd expect to find a bearing orange tree outdoors, but I know one that grows quite well, thanks to a good exposure and the fact that this orange tree is up against the south wall of a public sauna bath. The heat vents from the bath lead outdoors right by the tree so that not only does it receive plenty of sun, but it also gets the heat it needs to mature sweet oranges. Another example of a protected spot is a

Garden Layout 3/4 Acre

N
W — E
S

Permanent Asparagus and Artichoke Bed

Cole Crops (Broccoli, Kale, Cabbage)

Cover Crop (Peas, Scarlet Runner Beans)

Cold Frame

Roots and Greens (Onions, Leeks, Chard)

Roots and Greens (Lettuce, Carrots, Turnips)

Compost Bin

Tool Sheds

Rhubarb

Straw-Berries

Green House

Warm Weather Crops (Tomatoes, Summer Squash)

Long Season Root Crops (Parsnips, Salsify)

Winter Squash

Compost Making Area

Early Spring and Winter Garden (all crops except long season root and warm weather crops)

Herbs and Comfrey

Bush Fruits

Cypress Windbreaks   o—o—o—o—o—o
Fence   - - - - - - -

house I lived in in Eureka for a time. I had my tomatoes in pails along the south window of the porch. There was a community washer and dryer on that porch which provided heat for the plants all winter long.

Outdoors, remember that loose sandy soil warms up faster in spring and can be kept warmer longer in fall than heavy clay. The protected places are always in great demand so choose your vegetables carefully with an eye to what would be good to have there as winter comes. You might plant peas in the spring and kale in the fall for a long season of harvests. Or you might choose that spot for the tomatoes and peppers that you intend to nurse through the first early frosts. The north side of the garden is the place to plant perennials and tall growers like sunflowers and staked and trellised crops. That way they won't shade low growers. All the permanent fixtures such as compost bins, greenhouses, cold and hot frames, and storage sheds should be put off to the side on land that's not much good for crops. Under trees is often a good place for compost bins and sheds. Greenhouses and cold frames require less heat if placed in protected places like along the south wall of a house.

I figure the crops I plant in early spring will be followed by winter vegetables, so the first and last plantings make up one section of the garden. I reserve another section for crops that will take all season but which can be planted relatively early. Corn, parsnips, and salsify fall into this grouping. In other areas I plant roots and greens, often in alternate rows. Many of these will be succession crops. I don't plant everything at once because I couldn't possibly eat or sell everything at once. If I'm going to plant 200 feet of carrots I plant 40 feet first, follow that ten days later with another 40 feet, and so on until I've planted it all.

I reserve a section for cole crops and the crops that I will interplant among them. I like to keep the coles together because they have the same habits and require the same care (see chapter 10). I also set aside space for cucurbits, tomatoes, and peppers. They will all occupy the ground all season and need plenty of space. Finally there's a section that has a legume cover crop on it from the previous fall, which will remain until the next spring. The land sometimes needs a rest from constant crop production just as we need an occasional rest from our work.

I'm not going to go into the fine points of what to plant where. Other gardening books and the various state agricultural extension services have model garden plans for different square feet of space. At best they're rough guidelines that take little account of gardens that are geared to produce from every square foot of space for the entire growing season. However they have the advantage of telling the beginner how to lay out a plot in an orderly way. I suggest if you're a first or second time green thumber use them to get started, and then build to suit yourself as you gain confidence. I like what Sam Ogden says in his book, *Step-by-Step to Organic Vegetable Growing*, "I must confess that after forty years of gardening on the same plot I no longer draw out a plan for my garden." I haven't been gardening for forty years, but I must confess that my plans, like Sam's, come mostly out of my head as I go along. Then I fill in my plot sketches at the end of each day's planting. I encourage you to move toward the point where you have a feel for what's next. As I said in the beginning of this chapter, first have a vision for what you want to see and then work at it step-by-step. Somebody else's vegetable planting schemes are merely aids.

Seeds

With all the preliminary requirements out of the way it's time to work out seed requirements for the season. I begin by taking an inventory of seed on hand. Onions, parsnips, and corn lose their optimum viability after the first year so I test them before planting. I take a representative sample, put the seeds on a damp terry cloth one by one, roll up the cloth, and place it in a dark area at room temperature. I make sure the seeds stay moist until they germinate, and then I evaluate the results. If the germination percentage isn't close to the standard for that crop I discard the seed. I suggest the first few times you attempt seed tests that you use a known viable seed as a control so that if there's a failure you know for sure that it's because of the seeds and not because of your method.

Most seed is good for three to five years under cool, dry conditions, but to be on the safe side adjust your planting and buying so you never have seed left over more than a year. Estimating needs isn't too mysterious. I base my purchases on how many feet of row the packet or seed catalogs say a certain amount of seed will plant. The Agricultural Extension Service also provides bulletins on the subject as well as on how much of what to plant for the average family for fresh and processed vegetables. I follow the adage: Plant some for the birds, some for the bugs, some for your friends, and some for yourself.

Though I read a lot of catalogs I do business with only a few companies because it's cheaper for everyone that way. Postage and handling can make a packet of seed very expensive. I always order early in the season. I buy cole crops as early as December because I begin planting in January. I try to place my complete order before February 1. Any later means my order will be part of several million going to the catalog houses at the same time, and that translates into delay. More than once I've had to wait a month beyond the time I wanted seed because I ordered at peak season.

Keeping a Journal

Lastly, I keep a journal of everything I buy, when I plant, transplant, when seeds germinate, when they flower, when I begin the harvest, and the taste and quality of each crop. Recently I planted two types of edible-podded peas in a greenhouse. One germinated about two days before the other, and grew faster. The only reason I can tell you today that white-seeded dwarf sugar peas germinate quicker and grow faster than Oregon sugar pods is because I wrote down which was which and recorded their progress. All this information will help me select seed for next year's crops.

I also keep tabs on the work—plowing, raking, cultivating, weather conditions, rain and irrigation amounts, problems with bugs and disease, and what I did about them. I list which fertilizers I put where. A garden journal is indispensible. Most of us have a very hard time remembering what we did last week, let alone what we did a year ago, and if I had to rely strictly on my memory, I can promise you that I wouldn't be sure of too much of anything. There are few of us with the initial patience and discipline to keep up a journal, but I've found a few "I wish I had written that down's" will develop those qualities very quickly!

7
Growing
a Big Garden
in a Small Space

In America the prevailing philosophy for years has been "the bigger the better." I recently read that in areas where the 1930s dust bowls spurred farmers to plant shelter belts and windbreaks, today's big operators are tearing out those same belts, plus fencerows and everything else that interferes with gigantic equipment. The dust bowls may soon return.

I once visited the farm of a friend and he had a new $50,000 tractor. It was pulling a nine-bottom plow at the time but he assured me it would handle twelve in good ground. It did plow, disc, and harrow his field three or four times faster than the tractor his father used, but I question whether the speed is worth the debt. The tractor, to be economically feasible, needs more land to work than my friend has under cultivation. I wondered if the fencerows and woodlot would go to provide the needed acreage. Mechanical equipment not only takes a lot of space to make its use justifiable, but takes up a lot of space, period.

This latter point is what particularly concerns me. When you use hand equipment you can plant most vegetables more closely together than if you used machinery, making for more efficient land use. And, of course, tractors and equipment compact the earth every time they go down the rows. I'm not against power equipment per se, I just feel there's a point where the returns don't justify the capital invested in the machinery. I can grow more on an acre with only an initial rototilling each spring than any farmer can with all the power equipment at his disposal. And I believe I can do it—all costs considered—more profitably than he can.

My premise is that the small, intensive garden is more productive, more efficient, and more ecologically sound than any other kind of agriculture. And small size doesn't necessarily mean small profits for the market gardener. The most lucrative agricultural enterprise I've come across was a watercress farm in Hawaii that was operated almost entirely by hand. The owner made more money on a couple acres than some Western wheat farmers make on a thousand. I admit that some types of agriculture require large acreages, but my point is still that "small" doesn't necessarily mean "less." It definitely does mean astute management though, and that's an area I would like to introduce now and develop through the course of this book.

Mounded Beds

Ever since I read the book *Farmers of Forty Centuries* by F. H. King I've considered the idea of growing my vegetables in paddies or beds. The Chinese, by intensive methods, have been able to sustain up to twelve people per acre of arable land without lessening its productivity over the centuries. Compare this with the millions of acres of virgin soil that have been exhausted in a century by modern American methods.

Up until recently my own experiences with raised-bed agriculture were always negative. The beds required an investment in wood or some other material, and they always seemed to break apart after a few years. They dried out too quickly, and they crowded root zones on the perimeters. On the other hand, beds do have the great advantage of compartmentalizing vegetables. More important, if the beds are narrow enough so that you can reach to the center from either side, you can grow more food in less overall space. Instead of having a lot of rows with space between to walk in or cultivate, you plant the whole bed so the mature plants will be just touching

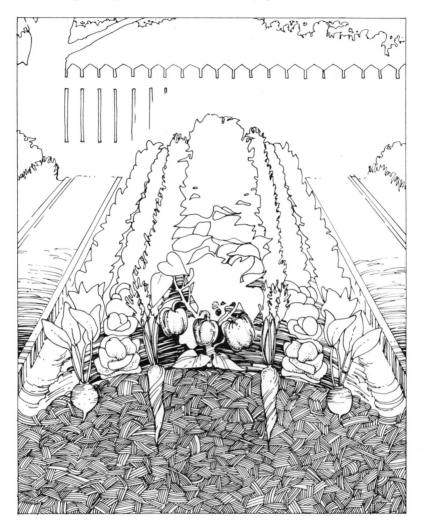

MOUNDED BED

each other. I never did like all that space between rows. In the beds everything seems to be more highly visible. It's as if you have more control. You can be starting the seeds of one vegetable as you're harvesting another in the same bed.

87

All these advantages finally led me to mounded beds, a millennia-old method that doesn't require raised beds. It goes well with row cropping, which I find very beneficial for certain kinds of gardening, and it's not so esoteric that you have to follow moon phases, make secret compost preparations, or ever use any tool beyond the spade and rake, though I realize all these things have their value.

To make a bed simply lay out east-west rows as wide as is comfortable for you to reach conveniently from the edge to the middle without having to put a hand down inside the bed to brace yourself. For me this means about a five-foot bed. Make the beds as long as you like. Next dig or rototill the ground as deeply as you can. I went down to three feet over several hundred square feet once, sifting rock out and incorporating leaf mold all the way. It was the only way I could figure to get a nonproductive piece of land productive. Most likely you won't get much deeper than twelve inches, but twenty-four would be better. Just make sure that the topsoil is still on top when you're done. Work compost or rotted manure into the top few inches of soil and shape the bed so that it forms a mound with slightly curved sides. (This is a small version of the Vermont hill farmers' axiom, "I wouldn't buy a piece of land that didn't stand up so I could farm both sides of it.") Actually, besides adding a little more planting space to your garden, this method also provides for better aeration. I like the sides and ends to be just a little lower than the pathway level. That way if you water too much by mistake or something disturbs the bed the soil will fall into the gutter and not into the path. I think a wood strip alongside the path edges is good to keep both path and bed in their respective places.

You can now plant any crop you want in any formation you want, including trellises or poles. Irrigation can be done by overhead perforated hose, oscillating or pulsating sprinklers, or by drip. As the years go by and you continue to improve the soil, you won't have much more to do every year other than work the old mulch and new fertilizer into the top four or five inches of soil, make the mounded beds, and plant—except, of course, to turn under cover or green manures. There is something to be said for not continually turning the soil upside down as we do with conventional plowing or spading, which is why I often cut off a cover crop at ground level. The decaying roots add humus to the lower levels, and provide aeration and food for a large earthworm and soil-microorganism population. You don't have to turn the ground over that deeply or that often in the organic garden, especially if you grow subsoiler crops every few years.

More Intensive Gardening Ideas

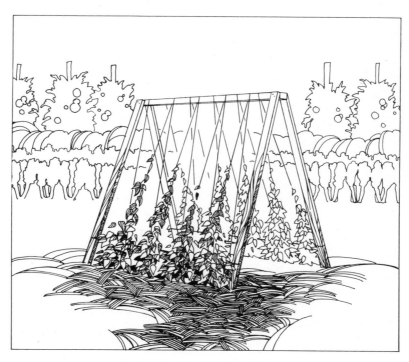

CHINESE LATTICEWORK

Another facet of intensive gardening is never to let anything sprawl when you have time and materials to stake or trellis it. This includes cucumbers, squashes, and melons. Except for the north end of the garden or where plants are growing along a fence, the Chinese method of making a triangular latticework and growing vine crops up through it is hard to improve. When the vines are just starting you can use the space for other crops that will be gone before the trellised vegetables shade them out. Radishes and leaf lettuce will even grow underneath a dense shade. I often grow beans on tripods; peas on trellises; tomatoes on stakes, in series of hog-wire rings, or on trellises.

I also intercrop, which is the way to get two crops from one space. I plant dry beans among corn because the former can use the corn stalks as trellises, while the

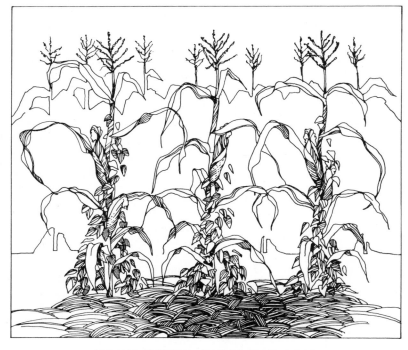

INTERCROPPING BEANS AND CORN

latter benefits from the nitrogen. Cucumbers will grow among sunflowers and yield sweeter fruit in partial shade during the heat of summer. These are instances of plants occupying different air or ground zones. Other plants grow closely together because they have root systems at different levels. You can plant lettuce right up to carrots. The first has a shallow root system, the other gets its nutrients from a moderately deep level. When I have the choice I always alternate carrots and lettuce rather than plant solid blocks of either.

Lastly, there's the continuous use of the cold frame or hotbed which I'll discuss in depth in the next chapter. If you have started crops ready to plant just prior to or immediately after a harvest, you can greatly extend the production capability of the land with frames because there's no wait for seeds to germinate and grow. This could mean getting an extra crop or two out of a well-fertilized and managed plot every season.

Obviously, operating an intensive garden is not a sudden thing. It takes years to develop timing, knowledge of vegetable habits, the techniques of intensive culture, and the soil. We in America have a very slim tradition to draw on, and few master gardeners to show the way. I've learned mostly by trial and error and by reading about what other gardeners have done. As a consequence I'm still a beginner in this area, and I present these ideas not as one who has mastered them, but as one who is learning that it doesn't take a giant parcel of land and a great capital outlay to be free of processed foods or to make an independent living on a homestead. It only takes a willingness to work with one's hands and with nature, to pay attention to the details of vegetable growing, and to realize that "big" doesn't have to mean units of space, but rather units of production in the space we have.

8
Cold Frames and Hotbeds

I put off building a cold frame for several years because I wanted glass sashes. They're the most durable, allow the greatest amount of light in, and retain heat well. During those years I started plants on window sills, on porches, or wherever I could give them some protection from the elements. It wasn't worth the wait. I eventually realized while my glass house was off in the dream future I was gardening here and now, and to do it better I needed the right equipment at hand. So I went out and bought some cheap six mil polyethylene plastic at a hardware store, wrapped it around a wood frame, and in a couple of hours I ended several years of

COLD FRAME

manipulating flats and peat pots from one inefficient location to another. I also extended my gardening season by a couple months for some vegetables.

Building Frames

If you've been delaying construction on a hot or cold frame because you wanted the "best" or were just unsure about their operation, my advice is don't. There's nothing mysterious or technical about using either cold or hot frames. Your state agricultural extension service most likely has plans for either along with explicit instructions for use in your area. The extension offices and the U.S. Department of Agriculture also offer simple greenhouse plans and instructions on how to use them.

A cold frame is simply a structure that affords plants basic protection from the elements. Add heating coils and you have a hotbed. (Actually, if you want to be technical, a hotbed is heated from somewhere beneath the soil surface, while it's the air that's heated in a hot frame.) Their uses are manifold. You can sow seed directly into the beds, or into flats or pots which will then be placed inside the frame for later transplanting. You can also sow such fast-growing crops as set onions, spinach, radishes, and mustard for direct use in early spring. Or you can start cucumbers or melons early and leave them in the frame (uncovered during good weather) for the rest of the season. Finally, frames are good for sowing greens and root crops that will grow and be harvested in winter.

If you plan on using glass the standard cold frame size is three by six feet. I finally did get a long glass frame and shortly after a group of children broke every panel. Now I use polyethylene. Mylar or fiberglass are longer-lasting, but they also cost more than polyethylene. When using plastic make sure it is well battened against "breathing" in the wind or it will wear out too quickly. Also, make provisions to remove it when it's not in use to extend its life.

The frame should be made out of some durable or rot-treated wood. I use redwood and think it's by far the best. In addition to its rot and insect resistance it has the property of being able to absorb great quantities of moisture and release it back in drier times, thus helping to maintain a proper humidity range. Some people, however, prefer cinder block to wood since it doesn't deteriorate and it allows you to cement the bed in place permanently.

The pitch back to front of a frame should be about one inch per foot. A standard frame sixteen inches high in the back and six feet wide should have a front ten inches high. If you have a south or east slope you might

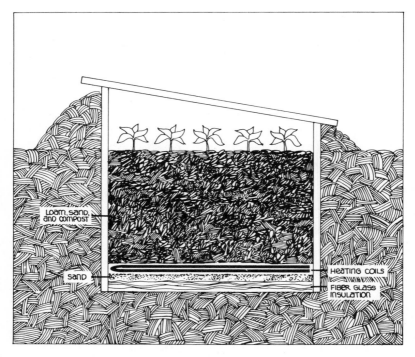

HOTBeD

want to cut your frame right into the bank to make use of the insulating properties of the earth. Otherwise it's a good idea to bank soil or thick mulch around the sides in autumn for winter protection.

The basic cold frame rests right on the ground over a soil that has been prepared six inches deep like a giant potting medium. If you're using peat pots you can excavate about three inches of dirt so the tops of the pots are at ground level. The hot frame sides should be buried a few inches.

There are lots of ways to build a hotbed. One is to remove eight inches of dirt, lay down a thin layer of fiberglass insulation, then an inch layer of sand, a heating coil, and six or so inches of a mixture of one-third loam, one-third sand, and one-third compost to bring it up to ground level. If you're planting in pots don't excavate more than six inches deep and refill with sand or dirt so the tops of the pots will stand at ground level. For crops that will spend their lives in the frame I suggest using overhead lights for early spring heat, and making a twelve-inch bed of loam, compost, and sand. Handle and fertilize as you would for any other crop. Place all lights and heating elements just the way your plans state to minimize scraggly growth.

Operating Frames

The three major considerations in operating any kind of frame are irrigation, ventilation, and heat control. Too much moisture will give many bacterial and fungus diseases an opportunity to spread. As a guide, see if there is condensation on the insides of the panes or plastic by evening if you watered in the morning. There shouldn't be. Naturally you want to be sure your plants aren't underwatered, so an occasional check with your fingers or trowel to test rates of penetration and uptake is also a good idea. It's best to either water with a sprinkler can or a very fine hose mist, and preferably with water that's close to the temperature of the growing medium to avoid shock.

In the cold frame, opening and closing the sashes determines the temperature. I use a notched block so I can open the frame in inch increments. Hopefully ventilation will do three things—admit fresh air without a draft, control humidity, and regulate temperature. The hotbed is the same except that on cold days a thermostat helps regulate temperature. On days when the air temperature will go above 70° I make sure to open the frame by mid-morning to avoid wilting, especially if I'm using pots. I also make it a habit to keep the frame open some every day that the inside temperature will stay above 50° for cool weather, and 60° for warm weather crops. This makes for hardier and more compact plants because without the constant "hot house" effect their growth is slowed a little. I close the frame in late afternoon when the sun begins to lose power.

I find it best to separate plants according to heat needs. This can be done by putting a divider in the frame and heating one portion, by opening or not opening certain panels, or by having different frames. Experience and experiment are the best teachers in this area. In the chapters on specific crops I'll give further recommendations about temperatures, frame uses, and the crops that go in them.

PART III:
Fruits and Vegetables to Grow

9

Basic Cool Weather Crops

Here on California's northern coast, I live in a fog-influenced climate. My gardens are subject to almost daily salt winds and cool weather. Such conditions make it hard to grow warm season crops. The ocean is only a few degrees cooler in the winter than in the summer, however, and it warms up even the coldest time of the year. Growers fifteen or twenty miles inland experience freezes that don't even faze my crops. The first expected frost is around December 15 and the last around mid-February. Sometimes there will be light frosts every night for a week, but they disappear quickly when the sun rises. Rarely is there anything more than a light frost. Together, these conditions make it almost perfect for me to grow the fifty or so vegetables I call "cool weather crops."

This large group of vegetables, most of them roots and greens, thrive in cool weather, withstand adverse conditions like rain, snow, and frost, and yield more abundantly than they would if the weather were warm. Though they come from at least nine different families they have many of the same broad requirements. A number of them grow year-around here, though very slowly in the winter. I build my garden around them.

They include all the cultivated members of the mustard family from kale and cabbage to rutabaga and radishes; the composite family, including chicory, lettuce, and artichokes; the edible lilies like asparagus; the edible alliums including onions and shallots; sorrel in the buckwheat family; beets, chard, and spinach of the goosefoot family; the peas and favas of the legume family; the commonly cultivated members of the parsley family including carrots, celery, and parsnips; corn salad of the valerian group; and potatoes of the nightshade family.

They are frost-tolerant to varying degrees. Some, like kale, withstand temperature dips into the teens. To give you an idea of the kind of temperature they prefer, the monthly average should range from a minimum 45° to a maximum 75°, with the best temperature in the 60° area. Rhubarb will even grow when the average is a touch above 30°.

Their seeds germinate in cool soil. Lettuce, for example, will germinate as low as 35°, and I've heard of spinach sprouting on melting ice. Most have shallow or moderate root systems compared to the extensive systems of warm weather crops like watermelons. Because their roots are closer to the surface they need to be irrigated frequently during dry weather. Many of them are leafy vegetables or roots like radishes that must be grown rapidly for best quality. They appreciate liberal applications of nitrogen since with the exception of the roots and properly inoculated peas and favas, they are heavy nitrogen feeders. I can safely plant them a couple of weeks before the last expected frost date. They should mature before the warm weather comes.

I begin as many as possible of them indoors because their hardiness means that I can set out started plants about the same time other gardeners are sowing seeds outdoors. The onions and garlic are so hardy that I set them out in the fall and they grow through the winter.

(Of course, you have to realize that the real winter along the north coast is not one of biting cold, but of driving rain. Gardening in southern Humboldt County, I've recorded over 125 inches of rain between October and May. This doesn't bother radishes or carrots, but tomatoes will speedily rot and die, even though the first frost date is a month away. In regard to cool weather crops, my West Coast situation is different than most of the United States except perhaps parts of the Gulf and Atlantic seaboards. For warm weather crops I pretty much hoe the same row as other gardeners. They're limited by frost; I'm limited by rain.)

Although my special climate conditions mean that you probably won't be able to grow as many crops during the summer as I do, you can grow most of them by making the necessary adjustments in planting time—it's basically a matter of starting about a month later than I do. With that understanding we can now look at the cool weather crops.

Fava Beans: Number One in My Cool Weather Garden

 I have a favorite cool weather crop. It grows all winter, improves the soil through the addition of nitrogen, helps eradicate tomato-wilt organisms as it decays, and yields a high protein fresh or storage crop. Although it's actually a vetch, the fava bean is its name. It's been highly regarded in Europe since antiquity when it was the only cultivated "bean," and it goes under various other names, including faba, windsor, broad, and horse bean.

I grow it because it produces a high protein (about 25 percent) crop in areas or at seasons too cool for other beans. It stores well and roasted and salted it makes an excellent, long-keeping, nutritious snack. The plants take about four to five months to mature and need cool weather most of the time, making it difficult to grow them in many places. However, in learning to get a crop going in the middle of winter I've worked out a way so that just about anyone who can sow seeds like radishes by March 1 can grow a good stand of favas, especially by using the quick-maturing dwarf garden variety now available from some seed houses.

Growing favas successfully hinges on two things: handling the seed correctly and preparing the ground the previous autumn. I like to use a plot that has just

103

been in brassicas, lime it for a pH 6–6.5, add rock phosphate at the rate of a half-pound per 100 square feet, and turn the soil over enough to get the cabbage mulch underground where it will begin decomposition. I rake the plot smooth and lay on a light mulch to protect the ground from the pounding winter rains.

At planting time in January and March (you'll have to plant in March if your ground freezes in winter), I watch the extended weather forecasts for a time that's supposed to be warm and dry for at least three or four days. Then I begin what I call the "Tom Becotte Never Fail Fava Plan."

For a couple years I'd been trying, with middling success, to get the right combination of weather, timing, and favas for an early crop. When Tom came to the Lighthouse Ranch he brought the idea of soaking beans (figure a pound for a fifty-foot row) in a bucket of warm water overnight.

"I've tried it, and it still takes forever for the beans to come up," I told him.

"You haven't tried what I'm going to do," he replied confidently.

The morning after soaking the beans he picked off all the dead "floaters," those seeds that come to the top of the water instead of sinking to the bottom. "This is what separates the high production experts from the unschooled weekenders," he said. "You've heard how good the Portuguese are with growing favas. Now I'm going to show you an ancient Italian version. I learned it from the former chief horticulturist to King Victor Emmanuel's court while playing bocce ball at the Monterrey wharf. . . ."

Tom's equally good at gardening, playing the piano, and telling stories. Wherever he got his plan, it worked, and I've used it since for a number of different crops. He rolled the seeds in a damp blanket to germinate, and while they were doing that we opened furrows two feet apart and an inch deep. When the sprouts were a quarter-inch long we inoculated them, which is simply coating the seed with a commercially prepared nitrogen-fixing bacteria strain according to the package directions. There was some discussion of this point that year.

"Did you inoculate last year?" Tom asked.

"Sure did," I replied.

"Did you use a vetch inoculant?"

"Sure did."

"I don't think you need to inoculate this year. The bacteria are already in the soil."

"I'll tell you what, Tom. For a 49¢ package that's going to cover all the favas we plant this year I'm going to do it. There's a principle here: Sow sparingly, reap sparingly."

"I have another principle," he answered. "Waste not, want not."

We didn't come to an agreement on the subject, but we did agree to lay each bean on its side, and cover firmly enough to insure a good contact between seed and soil. Then Tom had another suggestion. I had previously left the ground bare for the first several weeks of an early crop's life. He suggested a light application of a dark-colored heat-absorbing mulch like rotted sawdust. We tried it and it worked, helping both plants and ground through light frosts and hard rains.

With all the preliminaries out of the way we sowed one seed every inch and a half, and when they were two inches high thinned to three inches apart. We cultivated the soil to eliminate weeds, further loosen and warm the soil, and permit air penetration.

If my planting is in March rather than January I also apply a heavy mulch—usually seaweed—after the weather warms up. A little later the rains will have ceased and I'll have to irrigate. Favas like a lot of moisture, and I apply it whenever the top half-inch of soil dries out. They seem to be resistant to moisture-aggravated diseases like rots and mildews, but even so I prefer to do my watering on sunny days in the morning or early afternoon.

Sometime after four months the crop is ready. The seed pods, which follow pretty, dark-spotted flowers, look rather like bristles sticking out horizontally from the stalk and are borne from the bottom to the top. The variety I plant, Giant English, bears pods five inches long and an inch wide. There are four to five beans in each pod, some of them as big as a quarter across.

Determining the best time to pick is a matter of taste. I recommend two pickings—one of the bottom and one of the top half—when the bean just fills up its velvety seedpod, has a full, plump appearance, and tastes a little sweet rather than starchy. The bean will soon go to starch, but not as quickly as peas. You can eat them fresh, cook them, or freeze them. They do have a seed coating or skin that many people object to because of its toughness, but after cooking it's very easy to slip this skin off, or to mash it up with the rest of the bean when making fava bean loaf, a meat loaf-like main dish.

If you'd rather have a dry crop let the beans mature on the stalks. Along the coast I have to dry them indoors after shelling. Some people eat the very young pods like Chinese peas. My wife has prepared them in this way, but our conclusion is that there are better things to eat than immature fava pods. There is also a report that favas contain a toxic substance that disappears when the beans reach a mature green state. My family has suffered no ill effects from eating the immature pods, but I advise caution to others who might have a slightly different body chemistry.

When I've harvested the first crop I turn it under and let it sheet compost until I'm ready to plant garlic and onions. Meanwhile, in the beginning of July I start a second crop. I soak the seeds overnight and plant in the morning. I put this crop immediately under a heavy mulch to help retain moisture and to keep the ground cool. The beans will be ready before the first frosts hit the garden. In other parts of the country they will grow through a series of fall frosts, and providing the ground doesn't freeze, mature a crop in November by taking advantage of warm Indian Summer days.

A few Novembers before I really got involved with this crop I went over to Hydesville to visit a fellow named Jack Loffer who custom-makes knives in his garage. As I passed through his front yard on that first visit I noticed he had a garden instead of a lawn. Intrigued, I stopped to look. There were the usual lettuces and broccoli that will tolerate the moderate frosts of the flat ridge where he lived, but there were also favas. I asked him what he thought he was going to get besides a lot of leaves and maybe a few flowers since I didn't think any seed crop could develop in really cool weather.

"You bet they'll mature," he told me. "You take those Italian farmers down in the Loleta bottoms. They get a crop in December or January. I've been doing it for years. Start them out in early September. You get a harvest sooner or later the next year. You bet. Those favas stand up to a snowstorm."

I make a third planting in September, an option open only to other Pacific Coast gardeners and to those in the Deep South or extreme Southwest. This crop might go in after kale or onions and garlic, and will occupy the ground for the entire winter, taking advantage of the beautiful warm spells the West Coast receives almost every January.

Favas are humus and nitrogen builders if turned back into the soil as green manure or compost. I use them a great deal where other gardeners or farmers might use soybeans in rotation. I also use the favas' erect growing habit to plant greens or root crops in the spaces between the rows. For this purpose I open the spacing to thirty inches and plant the catch crop* down the middle,

---

*A catch crop is one that "catches" space and nutrients that otherwise might be wasted.

often in double rows six inches apart. Though I don't do this myself, small farmers can grow favas strictly as a green manure, turning them under when they're three months old. I mentioned this as a good practice if you're going to plant the plot to tomatoes. Potatoes, peppers, and eggplants are also subject to the same tomato-wilt that favas seem to counteract. One of the fava's alternate names—horse bean—indicates its value as a fodder, too, though I understand its use has been reduced in this country by improved vetches and clovers. Regardless, I find it to be an excellent all-around legume for the cool season—food for man, beast, and soil.

Peas

 I sing many of the same praises about peas that I do about favas—and some new ones besides. First of all, there are three ways to grow them: for their edible pods, for the fresh whole peas, and for the dried product. Second, there are tall-climbing, semidwarf, and dwarf varieties, so you can choose to trellis or not to trellis. Most important, the pea is the only high protein crop I know that you can plant a month before the last expected frost date, and harvest in about sixty days. In a world where balanced diets and protein are in short supply, the family that grows, eats, and gives away or sells this excellent legume can make a small, yet significant contribution to world health. Finally, pea hay is good animal feed, a fact that further recommends its production, especially when the nitrogen-rich manure is returned to the soil it came from.

Peas mature much faster than favas, but they aren't as hardy. For example, pea seeds—most markedly the wrinkled types—don't stand up to really poor weather conditions as well as favas. I don't plant them before March now as I've had too much difficulty with poor stands in February and near disasters in January. At the end of the growing season frosts damage pods and flowers. One year I planted in late October and got a beautiful stand. During a couple of warm weeks in January they flowered, but the cold weather returned and they never did bear peas. By contrast, favas will produce in such weather.

Peas like a soil temperature above 45°, and an average monthly air temperature in the low 60s. Just about everywhere in the country, except the extreme north or in high altitudes, the ground should be ready for peas around March 1 to 15. I open a V-shaped furrow about six inches deep and add three inches of compost and a light dusting of rock phosphate and limestone before covering with another couple of inches of dirt. You could add rotted manure in the same quantity but it's not quite as balanced as compost, and it's harder to come by. Peas will grow on any average or poor soil that's well drained, and leave it in better condition than it was, but a little assistance does help.

I didn't realize how much it helps until one day a neighbor stopped by just as I was about to plant peas.

"What do you use on them?" she asked, referring to the stuff I was sprinkling down a furrow.

"Rock phosphate." I knew peas needed this element abundantly to form pods and peas.

"That's all?"

"I'll probably add some lime."

"What are you going to do about nitrogen?" Her expression and tone of voice left no doubt in my mind that I was dealing with a woman who could not only hoe her own row, but mine too.

I began to wonder. What was I going to do about nitrogen? "I'm going to let the nitrogen-fixing bacteria manufacture all the plants need," I answered. "What would you do?"

In her very best instructional tone (this particular woman is a high school teacher as well as a gardener) she replied, "I always put manure right in the furrow when I plant."

That's nice, I thought, but most likely unnecessary.

But she had her reasons. Those nitrogen-fixing bacteria don't get going till later in the season, after the ground warms up. They're nearly inactive in cold ground, and they need time to build up in the nodules. If you don't have plenty of nitrogen for the peas at the beginning—to give them a fast start—they won't produce as well.

I tried it with bloodmeal instead of manure with good results. Now, no matter what variety I use or what kind of sowing arrangement, I add a nitrogen booster.

Speaking of varieties, the choice is stupendous, probably into the hundreds. For dwarf shell peas I suggest the fusarium wilt-resistant Thomas Laxton and Little Marvel, or Laxton's Progress No. 9, or the extra early strain of American Wonder called Nott's Excelsior. This last has been around for the better part of the century and is an old market gardener's favorite. It's ready in fifty-six days under ideal conditions, and has an acceptable flavor, something that can't be said of many of the smooth-seeded varieties. For the main season, Tall Telephone is a standard choice. This one will bear over a two- or three-week period if you keep harvesting the peas as they reach their peak. This is a considerably longer period than the early dwarfs will bear. Another main cropper is Wando. It's fusarium-resistant and reportedly stands hot weather better than the others. Among the edible-podded peas I've planted Mammoth Melting and Dwarf Grey, and find them both excellent. I generally plant the dwarfs because they don't need to be trellised. If I were going for "per unit of space" production the Mammoth is by far the better selection.

I usually trellis soup peas because I don't want the pods on the ground. The trellis makes good use of space and promotes high production. The type called Alaska Field is as good as any. In the early stages you can use it as a first early shell pea. I allow them to dry on the vine, give them a little further drying indoors because of the dampness of the climate, and shell by hand or threshing.

I start the season with field peas because they're most hardy. The easiest way to grow them or any tall pea is the way Tom Becotte devised in Loleta. Looking at his stand of field peas the first year he tried this method made me an instant convert. I had to know how he did it.

"You make your furrows six inches apart. Then you string a wire trellis between them. I've got wire nailed to a post every fifteen feet. It doesn't sag that way. I figure one wire twelve inches off the ground, and a couple more at three feet and five feet."

"How do you get them on the trellis," I asked, thinking of some snow peas I had that were wandering over the ground despite a convenient fence. His vines were so thick I couldn't see any support, only greenery. The plants were over five feet tall and beginning to grow down and sideways across the rows.

"I went down to the newspaper office and got all the twine left from the delivery bundles. All you have to do is unroll the ball—zigzag it up and down the wire from one end of the row to the other. Some of this cheap kite string works well too. The peas from one row fall over the peas from the other row after they start growing. They kind of naturally grab the twine and start going up."

I wanted to know what kind of spacing he used. There barely seemed room to get down the aisle.

"I've got forty inches between the posts. You can still get down the rows and there's no wasted growing space."

That's the way I've been growing tall peas ever since, figuring a half-pound of seed per fifty feet of row.

About a week after the smooth varieties are in the ground—whether they're for soup or fresh eating—it's time to plant the first wrinkled peas. These late varieties are generally sweeter than early dwarfs. I lay out my rows at eighteen inches for dwarf sugar peas and space the peas at one inch. The idea is to sow them so thickly that they will hold each other up.

The best advice on pea growing I ever heard was "give them a quick start and continuous growth." Compost and soaking seed overnight does the first; cultivation and watering accomplishes the second. Because the ground is cold in spring it needs to be warmed up by turning it over and exposing it to the sun. I don't bother cultivating the soup peas except to control weeds when the plants are about two inches high, but I start the sugar peas out with deep cultivation. (By deep I mean about four inches down and six inches away from the plant when the plants have been up for a few days.) I follow this initial cultivation with a second (two inches deep to within six inches of the plant) two weeks later, and a third two weeks after that. Later, when the weather is warming up, I put on a mulch. It's important to get a feel for where the root zone is so that you don't chop into it (this goes for all other vegetables as well), although I have a theory that perhaps a few severed roots stimulate production in seed-bearing plants. I'm still experimenting with the concept, and until I know better my judgment (unless you want to experiment too) is to cultivate carefully near the roots.

Peas appreciate water throughout their growing period. Some people go to great lengths to see that they get it, like sowing them at the bottom of six-inch deep furrows and drawing the soil in as the plants grow up to insure a deep drying-resistant root system. My advice: water if the ground shows signs of drying. Mulch well. The critical watering time is as the pods are forming. Make sure the soil is moist, but not wet up to the time the peas are well formed in the pods.

For continuous production throughout the spring, either plant different varieties with different maturity dates, or if you plant only one fresh-eating type as I do, sow a section of row every ten days. Schedule the last one to mature around the first week of July if you live in a hot summer area. Since I live in a cool weather climate I continue right up to September. Elsewhere plant around the first week of August using an early dwarf variety.

There's a narrow time range in harvesting edible-podded peas. I used to work at a natural foods Chinese restaurant, and did all the fresh produce buying in San Francisco's Chinatown. The cook wanted me to bring back pods that were just beginning to swell. He claimed that they were tenderest at that point, and I agree. However, the very best snow pea—the exceptionally sweet one—has begun to fill out the pod just a little. The cook explained the only way you can tell when that point is, is to taste the peas every day after the pods begin to swell. One day they'll taste incredibly sweet, and you'll know the right type of pea to look for. This point is so delicate that almost immediately afterward the pods begin to get objectionably tough. Chinese cooks would prefer to have all their peas at this sweet, crunchy point of perfection, but to be on the safe side—considering shipping, marketing, and storing—pick them early while they're definitely tender, and forget about that perfect sweetness. Such nuances, the cook assured me, were for home gardeners or the owners of commercial Chinese vegetable gardens, whom he visualized dining continually in opulent oriental splendor—every vegetable picked at its prime and cooked barely enough to combine its flavor with those of the other ingredients.

I carry what I've learned about snow peas over to shell peas too, taste-testing them about the time the peas look like they've filled the pods. Once the peas reach full size the sugar begins to change to starch. At the taste peak shell them as fast as possible, avoid washing, and either eat them within an hour or two or process, preferably by freezing. About 200 feet of row should be adequate for the average family. If you miss the peak with either edible pod or shell green peas, let them mature and you'll have dry peas for winter soups.

Once the harvest is in you can feed the hay to livestock, compost it, or turn it under. Late cabbage is a good follow-up crop for early peas as it appreciates the nitrogen.

If you go in for companion planting you can try radishes, carrots, cukes, corn, or beans with peas. I've grown late corn and peas together with great success. The rows should not be closer than thirty inches. Plant five peas in a circle about five inches from the corn after the latter is up and growing. Thin to the best three peas. Interplanting double rows of carrots with double rows of peas is a nice way to provide more room for maneuvering between the peas without sacrificing space.

Finally, save the best seeds by picking the earliest, tastiest, most prolific vines and letting the pods dry. After hand-shelling and sorting out the runts I spread them out for further drying indoors. Then I store them in cardboard boxes. The seed should last three or more years.

Potatoes

Most garden books will tell you to skip potatoes if you have a small garden. They're cheap to buy commercially, they're subject to too many pests and diseases, they take up too much space, and they're fattening. I'm going to tell you differently. Commercially grown potatoes, from seed to store, spend their lives getting doused, dosed, sprayed, and dusted with lethal chemicals from aldrin and formaldehyde to sevin and vapam, plus the two most dangerous of all—mercury bichloride and suspensions of organic mercury for the control of rhizoctonia and scab. You don't want to eat those potatoes if you can help it. You want to grow your own. And raising your own will give you something you can't buy in the store: that's the tender, sweet new potato.

Potatoes have a lot of advantages. In soil high in humus they're quite resistant to common diseases and pests. They're not really fattening—it's mainly the things we put on our potatoes that make us fat. They contain respectable amounts of vegetable protein and vitamin C, plus traces of other important vitamins and minerals. They store from one season to the next. Twenty feet of row per person in a family should be adequate. They're easy to grow and I've settled on two methods of growing them, depending on the availability of raw materials.

For the best and easiest way I'm indebted to my friend, the schoolteacher, who taught me a variation of the Ruth Stout "gardening without an aching back" method. My friend uses raised beds (her first laborsaving ploy was to get her husband to build the frames and truck in all the soil ingredients), but it will work on the ground as well. She works a two-inch layer of compost into the top few inches of soil, tosses on a couple-inch layer of partly decomposed leaves (that would be last autumn's leaf fall for a spring planting), and lays the spuds on top.

"You'll notice that I'm sprinkling on enough compost to cover each seed. I am not covering the whole plot with more compost," she instructed as we sowed seed potatoes one spring day. "Next we'll lay on the hay."

Woman's ingenuity and man's power actually put down a twelve-inch blanket of hay that day. The raised bed looked very neat and dirt-free (some accomplishment in a garden!), like a well-kept house. "My potatoes come out clean. No scrubbing. I simply rinse them off," was her triumphant conclusion.

I might add potatoes grown this way are also extra resistant to disease. Many of the pathogens that attack tubers and stems thrive in moist soil, but with the mulch method the tubers are relatively dry because they're above the general soil surface. The roots, which need moisture, are in the decomposing leaf mold or in the soil. The only difficulty with this method is that it takes a lot of leaves and mulch.

When I don't have enough mulch at potato time I plant the traditional way, four inches deep and nine inches apart in the rows that are two feet apart. I add compost at the rate of a wheelbarrow load every ten feet. As the vines begin to grow I progressively draw the soil around them so that by mid-season the big bushy plants are growing on ridges on a wide, shallow V-shaped furrow which I fill with mulch. In throwing the dirt up around the stems I'm careful not to go deep or close to the plants because they're shallow-rooted and easy to damage. When I've finished this "hilling" the tubers are eight to ten inches deep.

Potatoes should not precede or follow tomatoes because they're subject to many of the same diseases and pests. I never lime the sections of garden where I grow them because scab all but disappears at pH 5. Crops like chicory, endive, shallots, sweet potatoes, and watermelon grow successfully in soil where the pH is low, so use them in your potato bed rotations.

I'm convinced that high humus content is the greatest safeguard against the fifty or so pests and diseases that cause serious damage to commercial crops. I live adjacent to an area where commercial farmers use many of the chemicals I mentioned earlier. I've taken potatoes gleaned from their fields and planted them in my organic soil and to my knowledge I haven't lost a single plant to bugs or sickness. However, I do not recommend the use of uncertified seed. I suggest you start with whole certified potatoes, choosing a blight-resistant main cropper like Kennebec. Norgold is a good second choice, and for early potatoes use Norgold Russet. Pontiac is the standard among redskins. The "certified" label means

116

the sack of potatoes you buy does not carry certain diseases. It's always more expensive to buy certified seed, and always cheaper in the long run. Using my seed method will mean about ten pounds of seed per 100 feet of row.

For economy's sake you may want to plant as many eyes as you can from the potatoes you buy the first year, but afterwards you'll want to be selective and develop your own strain. You can do this in the following way. Each potato has a blossom end where most of the eyes are concentrated, and a stem where the potato was attached to the mother plant. About a month before planting time select well-shaped, shallow-eyed, medium-sized spuds, and cut off the last third of the stem end. This end has eyes but they don't perform as well as those from the blossom end. I cut the blossom end so that I get one or two eyes per seed. Too many eyes per seed produces foliage, not tubers. An expensive, but easy alternative is to slice the potato lengthwise into quarters. The starchy portion is a food supply for the beginning plant. Just be sure to remove all eyes but one or two.

I now place the seed, which is merely a generous hunk of potato with one to three eyes in it, in a sunny frost-free place for a couple of weeks to heal and green.

I learned an interesting extension of this method while driving south out of Half Moon Bay late one winter. A sign along the highway said, "Potatoes for Sale." I stopped, thinking I'd get a better deal than what the supermarkets offered. The old man who came out of the barn said there weren't any eating spuds left, but he had some seed potatoes he was giving away. I followed him into the barn where a few sacks laid shriveled and green in a corner. While I dug around for some nice specimens he returned to his work. That's what caught my eye.

"What are you doing there?" I asked.

His English was very broken, but his plan was

ingenious. "Sprouting potatoes. This is for me. Not for the farm. I will have potatoes to eat very soon."

He was taking cut potatoes that apparently had healed a few days and putting them in large flats that had about an inch of sand on the bottoms. Each potato was pushed up next to its neighbor. When the flat was filled he covered it to the brim with more sand and watered. "I put them in warm place. In two weeks you come back. Potatoes then have roots and sprouts. They are ready to plant."

It was a marvelous plan, one that here along the north California coast produces foliage a foot high in late March outdoors unprotected. The idea, geared to local weather conditions, will work anywhere. Later in the season it's a good way to have your potatoes going strong when you follow another crop in succession.

Another season I planted a 100-pound sack of certified Norgolds, some of which had stem sprouts fifteen and sixteen inches long because I bought them at a closeout for a cheap price. I carefully cut the potatoes into seeds, breaking off excessive stems, and then planted in moist soil about eight inches deep. By keeping the seedbed moist, instead of dying back, most of the stems put out leaves and I had a nearly instant stand. I don't advocate such radical procedures, but I hope it indicates just how much you can manipulate potatoes.

Set out your potatoes about two weeks before the last expected frost date (that's early April for me). If you want lots of smaller sized potatoes reduce the spacing in and between the rows. If you want larger spuds, increase the spacings. Potato seed will go through frosts, but after the foliage breaks through the surface it can only stand light nips, so protect emergent vines if a harsh cold snap comes. If vines are frosted, a vigorous seed will send up more stem to replace the lost parts. I try for the early crop, even chancing some spells of bad weather, as the earlier the crop, the less danger from potato pests.

As a companion vegetable I suggest garlic. It repels

bugs and apparently gets along well with potatoes. I plant cloves every few feet right along with the potatoes. I've read that nightshade will attract potato bugs away from potatoes, and that the bugs will subsequently gorge themselves on these weeds. In California I have nightshade, but no bugs; in Washington I had bugs but no nightshade to test this companion theory (I ended up handpicking the bugs). If you ever have both at once perhaps you can put this tip to good use.

Growing potatoes need good aeration and cultivation. A well-aerated soil is one that is well drained, but retentive of moisture because of the humus content and combination of sands, silts, and clays. This is the opposite of a soil that gets soggy after an irrigation and is a breeding place for pests like nematodes. Cultivation is a practice you can skip with the mulch method, and one that comes naturally as you hill up the vines in the second method I described. Water as the top inch of soil dries out in conventional beds. With a mulch bed it's time to water whenever the bed layer of mulch is showing drying signs. I do my last deep watering no later than a week after the majority of my vines have flowered.

The appearance of flowers signals the time to dig new potatoes. Around Loleta and the Ferndale bottoms where the Eel River meets the ocean there are several big potato farms, so folks have picked up a lot of spud savvy. For instance, an old-time Portuguese dairyman asked me one day if I were going to eat the new potatoes in my garden. I didn't know what he was talking about.

"New potatoes. You know. They're about this big," he said, making a gesture with his thumb and forefinger to indicate something about the size of a quarter.

I thought maybe he meant Irish potatoes, like the little ones you buy in a can.

"No. No. New potatoes," he repeated.

I was growing my spuds in dirt that season. He moved the mulch and with his fingers carefully dug down into the soft earth directly beneath the spot where the stem surfaces. I thought for sure he was going to ruin the plant.

"Here. Here's one. Eat that." He handed me a potato about the size of a nickel. "Go ahead. Eat it."

Dubiously I took a bite. Meanwhile he was digging for more. The potato tasted crisp and sweet—very sweet when you consider my taste buds were set for the starchy flavor of a mature potato.

"New potatoes. Salad potatoes, some folks call them. You get them when the flowers bloom." He paused to eat a few. "Don't hurt the plant none to eat them either."

Such was my introduction to what I now consider one of the all-time garden delicacies. If all I had was a postage-stamp garden on a city lot I would still plant a few hills spaced at four inches. When the new potatoes were ready I would harvest them, pull the vines, and plant a warm weather crop.

Harvest is when the vines die back. The soil should be dry. I mark the sturdiest vines while they're green, and then select seed for the next year from the heaviest yielding of those marked. They don't have to be the earliest to mature, but they should be in the first quarter of the crop. A lot of people leave their potatoes in the ground after maturity, but a rain could come and damage the crop. The best seed and storing potatoes come from tubers that are dug immediately after the vines die back in ground that has been allowed to dry out. Let them cure in the sun for a couple hours, then store in a cool, dark, moderately moist place. If light strikes the tubers during storage they can "green," producing a poison called solanine which is harmful to humans. If the storage area is too warm the tubers will sprout.

Early potatoes are not the main keepers. For the winter crop plant anywhere from early June to early July, depending on the variety and the first frost date. They should be ripe at the first killing frost. Handle this second planting exactly like the first one. The potatoes should last until spring—unless you're a confirmed baked-potato eater like I am!

Lettuce:
Queen of the Salad Bar

One of the grand equations of the vegetable world is: salad equals lettuce. Every gardener I've ever met grows lettuce, and every green salad I've ever eaten in a restaurant, with a few cabbagy exceptions, has contained it. It's as universally popular today as it was with the Chinese over a millenium ago, with the Romans and Greeks before them, and with the Egyptians even earlier. Along with radishes, it's probably the easiest and hardest vegetable to grow. I say easy because just about any viable lettuce seed placed in the ground, kept from being choked by weeds, and given some water will come to eating size. Hard, because the crisp, flavorful, tender, and mild-tasting vegetable we all relish requires some very knowledgeable attention to variety, timing, fertilization, and cultural practices.

To begin there are four main types of lettuce. In ascending order of ease of culture and tolerance to heat they are: the crisp-head types characterized by various strains or derivatives of Great Lakes; the loosehead or butterhead types originated by Jack Bibb in Kentucky in the last century, including Bibb and Boston; the looseleaf types of which Black Seeded Simpson is the most highly regarded and also least heat-tolerant; and the cos or romaine, characterized by upright (celerylike) growing habits, heat tolerance, and toughness. I've grown them all and my preference is for the butterheads, specifically Bibb. The cos lettuces, though highly touted by some as a gourmet delight, are easy to grow and

121

heat-hardy, but they are also exceptionally unnote-
worthy as far as taste goes.

I start lettuce in cold frame flats in January, but
elsewhere I suggest you begin six or seven weeks before
the last average frost date. My standard potting mixture
is one-third sifted compost, one-third clean sharp sand,
and one-third thoroughly rotted sawdust or peat moss. I
used to sow broadcast but now I put a seed one inch in
either direction. This saves me the trouble of one thinning operation. My first early choice is Black Seeded
Simpson. This is among the best of the leaf lettuces and
matures in about forty-five days, which means you can
actually begin eating the thinnings in about twenty days.
I plant Bibb at the same time. The seeds should sprout in
three to seven days if the soil temperature is at least 50°.

There are a lot of theories about transplanting lettuce and other crops. I sum up mine in this way.
Transplanting checks growth. Do as little as possible and
do it when the plants are as young as possible. Every
time you move a plant from one environment to another
you break off roots and root hairs, and the more developed a plant is the more it suffers. Growth slows
considerably while the plant repairs the root system.
With lettuce and other plants that I move from a sheltered location to the outdoors I transplant either one or
two times. (That's either from flat to field, or from flat to
flat to field.) Flat to field would be my first choice, but
unfortunately the root system usually reaches the bottom
of the flat and gets tangled before it's time to set the
plants out. One solution for plants that won't go into the
field for six weeks after sowing is to use deep flats and
space them farther apart, but this calls for great care in
growing and in transplanting. An easier method, then, is
flat to flat to field. When the seedlings are two inches tall
I transfer them from one flat to another and use wider
spacing, say three by three inches. After additional
growth I set them in the field. Such plants usually have
stockier root systems and more compact growth, both of

which are very important. An artifically warmed plant, especially one under glass or plastic, can get very weak and leggy.

I prepare the field with every possible enhancement to growth, following the lead of a lettuce grower friend whose experience in the warm Hawaii climate makes his counsel extra valuable.

Kimo called me one day to come see him work firsthand. He had already irrigated the field the day before and had also watered the transplants with a fish emulsion solution. "A couple days ago I blocked the plants—cutting the soil in the flats into squares," he explained. This is something like cutting a cake, keeping a plant in the center of each square. "You have to keep a ball around the roots to reduce shock. Unless you cut them in advance the roots will be all tangled up when you transplant and you'll rip them up and the soil will fall off."

I helped him lift each square "ball" out of the flats with a putty knife and place them in the furrow.

"We're coming to the critical part," he then told me. "Lettuce transplants easily if you press the soil around the ball, but you have to be careful not to scrunch the roots or they can't breathe. But if you press too lightly there's air pockets around the roots and they die from lack of contact with moist earth."

Finding that right balance isn't hard, but it does take a certain amount of attention and feel. Once you've got it, though, your plants grow much better. From several years experience working with beginners who usually pack the soil around transplants too tightly, I know that Kimo's advice, faithfully followed, can spell the difference between a crop that drags along and one that seems to leap to maturity.

Now let's return to the chilly spring mainland and backtrack a little, imagining it's the average last frost date in your area. For the previous ten days the lettuce has been in the cold frame and unless it was raining or the weather was excessively cold it was directly exposed to the elements. If the nights were exceptionally warm the top was left off the frame during the last few days and the watering schedule was reduced. The exposure to the elements and the reduction in water is a twofold way of hardening off plants, or preparing them for garden conditions. This creates a slight check in growth during which the plant stores carbohydrates in plant tissue that will be used to overcome transplanting shock. Five or six days before setting them out I blocked the plants, which forced them to develop feeder root systems close in around the main root.

I prepared the way in the field by adding a wheelbarrow full of compost to every fifteen feet of row. To this I added around a half-pound each of bloodmeal and dolomite. Lettuce requires a lot of nitrogen for fast growth. I broadcast the lime over the whole plot before adding the compost and bloodmeal as part of my continuing program to maintain slightly acid soil. This step is unnecessary where the pH is naturally near the lettuce's neutral preference.

With the plot watered the afternoon before, and the furrows opened so that one side is vertical, I'm ready to transplant. I hold the root ball against the furrow wall with one hand and with the other I trowel dirt up to and around the plant. When I'm done it's resting level in the bed. I space the Simpson at four inches, and later thin to eight inches. I start the Bibb and all other heading lettuces at four and a half inches and thin to nine. After covering the ground with a very light protective mulch I sprinkle on the very dilute fish emulsion solution.

Optimum quality lettuce will have unchecked growth once in the permanent bed and will mature before hot weather. I insure this by watering and cultivating, and by adding a deep mulch just as soon as the plants are established. I don't think side-dressing with a nitrogen fertilizer is necessary on rich organic ground because too much nitrogen makes tasteless, easily wilted leaves just as too much water makes a puffy head. The soil should be like a wet towel that's been wrung out in contrast to one that's dripping wet.

I like to set out early transplants between wide-spaced cauliflower and cabbage rows. I make it a point to interplant carrots with lettuce that I sow directly outdoors: two rows of carrots, one row of lettuce, etc. Not only do I use space that would otherwise be idle, but carrots and lettuce enhance each other's growth.

About the time I transplant I make additional sowings of Bibb and Simpson, and add some rows of Great Lakes. These will mature in forty-two to forty-six, fifty-five to seventy, and eighty to ninety days respectively. I repeat the outdoor sowings monthly up to September 1. After that I plant only leaf lettuce up to November 1 because it's hardier in cold weather and rain than the heading types.

In central Washington where the weather gets hot and dry in summer my second outdoor sowing was somewhat different. I sowed Great Lakes, Prizehead, and Hot Weather, a very decent variety for long-standing summer growth. In hot climates during the summer the leaf types like Prizehead and the slow bolting heads like Hot Weather are about the only choices, unless you want to set up lath shades or netting to stop the noonday sun.

I learned this the hard way one summer. The circumstances are a little hazy, but I think my plan was to have about 100 fresh heads of Great Lakes lettuce on hand for an August wedding. The weather probably got hot (for the coast 80° is a scorcher) while I was away for a few days. Though I may have forgotten the circumstances I'll never forget the sight that awaited me. Almost all those heads that had looked so fine just a few days before now sported what I call the "pagoda look." Right out of the middle of the head was tier upon tier of tiny leaves supported by a tough stalk. At a point about a foot and a half above the ground, flower heads were rapidly developing. The sad fact is regular lettuce will bolt in summer unless given lots of protection and prayer. Furthermore, lettuce, when it gets old or after hot weather arrives, tends to get tough and bitter. So stick to the specially bred summer types, or try the leaf or cos varieties. Regardless, no summer lettuce will have the taste or quality of the cool weather types, even if you erect shades and use extra deep mulches and lots of water. Acceptable, yes; great, never.

Spinach: Conqueror of the Cold

 Lest there be any tears of grief when it comes to spinach growing I want to preface my observations with an excerpt from the California Agricultural Extension Service's pamphlet, *Home Vegetable Gardening*, "Late spring planting will probably 'bolt'. Winter plantings may be affected by downy mildew. Swiss chard is more practical for home gardeners than spinach." So why bother to grow spinach? Because, as my wife says, the substitutes like New Zealand spinach and mustard spinach notwithstanding, nothing tastes like the real thing. Furthermore, it's extremely high in vitamin A and vitamin C, higher in protein than most other greens, and cooked it has an appreciable amount of available calcium.

Experience has taught me I can overcome cultural difficulties by working within the limitations of the crop. Spinach is the quickest of the greens to bolt. Warm weather and long days trigger seed stalk production. On the other hand, it enjoys those seasons of the year that literally kill many other vegetables, and the disease problems that commercial growers have become relatively insignificant in the organic garden.

The secrets of spinach growing really aren't too mysterious. All you need is an organically tended, well-drained soil, rich in nitrogen, a pH in the near-neutral range, cool weather and short days, and rapid growth. The soil can't be too rich. If you could afford to plant in pure, well-balanced compost, spinach would probably develop to its full potential. Barring that, rotted manure or compost at the rate of ten pounds per ten square feet of row, mixed into the top couple inches of soil along with a sprinkling of bloodmeal and enough dolomite to show pH 6, but not more than pH 6.7 will go a long way in helping to turn out quality spinach. The lime application should be dolomite because this crop can suffer from magnesium deficiencies as the pH approaches neutrality. I wouldn't put any lime on a soil that was pH 6 or more because such soils, except under the rarest circumstances, have sufficient available calcium. Whatever fertilizer I add, I never mix it deeply because spinach, like lettuce, is a shallow-rooted crop. Its root system will pick up nutrients near the surface and those that leach downward from the surface through rain or irrigation, but if the nutrients are mixed deeply, they will be unavailable to the plants at the outset and might possibly leach out of reach of the root system before the plants could ever use them. This can happen with all shallow-rooted vegetables, especially when the nutrient is nitrogen.

Happily, cool weather and short days coincide. (Cool weather and long days won't do at all.) I tried planting in partial shade in June, mulching heavily and hoping the ocean fog would keep my plants cool enough to mature in August. The ground stayed cool but something in the spinach told it it was the season of the longest days of the year—and the crop bolted. By the way, don't associate cool and short with shady. Spinach actually prefers the sun, and it's in full sun and cool weather that you have the least trouble with diseases and pests.

I wait for a break in the February rain, prepare the ground quickly when it's dry enough to work, and sow seed about a half-inch deep in rows twelve inches apart at the rate of one seed per inch. At this rate an ounce of seed should sow 100 feet, which is about all the average family would need in a year for fresh and stored use. When the plants are two inches tall I thin to four inches in the row. I begin picking outer leaves for salads about a month after sowing. The whole plants are ready about two weeks after that. Some people make one or two plantings and pick the outer leaves. I find that the plants don't stay in peak condition long enough to make leaf picking the norm. Better to harvest the whole plants as soon as possible, and depend on succession planting for a continuous supply. For fresh eating I cut them in the mid-morning while the leaves are still at their crispest.

What a difference between fresh spinach and the canned product. I once opened a can of cooked spinach to feed a young friend of mine as the vegetable dish with dinner.

"What's that stuff?" he asked as I dumped a sodden mass of greens into a saucepan to heat.

"Spinach. It's good for you. It's got lots of vitamins and minerals."

"I don't want any."

"What do you mean, you don't want any? You haven't even tried it," I countered.

"I don't have to try it. I can *see* it. It's yucky."

I resorted to the age-old "This is the stuff Popeye eats every time Popeye needs super energy" argument as I spooned some on his plate. I had to admit it, though, it looked like a bunch of weeds that had long since wilted and gone through a couple of rains.

"I don't like Popeye either," was all I got for my trouble as my friend proceeded to push his serving to the side.

That was the end of that—except, of course, for the fact that I dutifully ate a large portion of the near-tasteless greens to be an example. He was right—they were miserable—and I've never bought a can of spinach in the eight years since. Why should I when fresh homegrown leaves picked the way I've described are an entirely different (not to mention much better) vegetable? I even believe homegrown leaves would turn the hearts of America's children back to spinach at first taste.

I continue with plantings up to May 15, and resume again around September 1. If I lived in a winter-freeze area I would concentrate about half my spinach planting (to freeze and can in a slack time) on light soil with a southern exposure about the time the first two inches of topsoil had thawed. The rest I would put out in ten-day intervals up to a week before the last expected frost date, but no later than May 1.

Watering is a cautious task because the two problems that affect this crop most—dampening off and downy mildew—both appear under moist conditions. To prevent these diseases I don't sow when there's a possibility of rain, and I don't draw mulch right up to the plants. I also avoid the damper mulches like seaweed in preference to wood chips and hay. Spinach likes water, but confine your watering to sunny mornings so the crop will have a chance to dry off. You can further thwart the problem of downy mildew by keeping spinach in a four-year rotation.

In October you can start two late crops. Frost will halt the first one, but it will resume growth in the spring as the ground thaws out. Grow the other in an open cold frame until the beginning of freezing weather, then cover the frame except on warm days and you'll have greens into December. Along the north coast my October crop produces very slowly for several months without cover if I pick only the outer leaves. Winter is the only time I endorse leaf picking.

Longstanding Bloomsdale (longstanding means the variety is slow to bolt), Nobel or Giant Thick Leaved (a favorite for canning), and King of Denmark are standard varieties. I stick with Bloomsdale and Nobel year-around, but there is a variety called Eskimo that is

129

specifically bred for overwintering. All types are very easy to transplant, but I never bother unless dampening off or some other problem arises and I don't get quite the stand I want. The fact that this hardy member of the goosefoot family overwinters, or can be planted extremely early in the spring outdoors, makes starting indoor flats a waste of time. On the other hand, its very hardiness makes it an ideal choice for production in the winter cold or hot frame.

If you're saving seed, pick the fastest growers, then select to taste. Of the ones you like choose those that send out seed stalks last. That way you'll be able to improve your spinach crop—and your spinach eating—year after year.

The Onion and Its Relatives

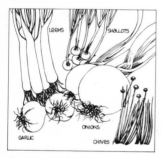

For such a common plant the onion and its relatives have enjoyed a long and distinguished history. One Egyptian mummy was found with an onion in hand and in China garlic is so ancient it has a separate character all its own. But my favorite allium story is the complaint of the Israelites after Moses led them out of Egypt into the wilderness toward the Promised Land, "We remember . . . the leeks, and the onions, and the garlic, but now is our soul dried away; there is nothing at all save this manna to look upon." I doubt that today there are as many people who take such an exalted view of the onion family. Most of us are concerned with smelling sweet, and the onions and garlics aren't much help in that area. Edible alliums have lots of other worthwhile characteristics, though, and I'm all for a return to growing and eating more of them. After all, if we all ate raw garlic nobody would notice anyone else had garlic on the breath.

The species I'm going to discuss are all closely related and have practically the same cultural needs. They will grow in flowerpots as well as any indoor flowering plant if kept cool (they thrive in a 60°- to 65°-range, but will tolerate the low 70s), and will reward growers with food as well as big, round, usually purple flowers. Outdoor culture is as easy as indoor.

Onions   There are four basic types of onions. The first is the bulb onion. It comes in mild forms for fresh eating and in pungent forms for cooking. Next is the scallion, or bunching onion, which grows about ten inches high and a half an inch thick without forming a bulb. This is the "green onion" that's served in relish trays. Any leek or bulb onion of that same general size can pass for a scallion. Third are the top multipliers or Egyptian onions. They look like green onions except that they grow little bulbils, or buds on the tips of their leaves, which when planted yield more onions. They make good greens and grow well indoors. Lastly is the potato onion, which is a root and stem multiplier.

When I moved into one of my gardens there was a clump of potato onions that appeared as if someone had spilled a packet of seed. They were growing bunched up so I divided all the plants. They were loosely attached by the roots, but I still thought they were regular onions. In late summer I had a very long row of onion bunches. They make good scallion substitutes, are perennial, and lend themselves to transplanting for companion work at any season. To eat, lift as much of the clump as you need, rinse quickly, and remove the tough outer skin. Every garden should have this onion because it's both easy to grow and very useful.

Getting back to bulb onions, there are three ways to grow a crop. One is from started plants. Growers in

Texas specialize in preparing young plants for sale to northern gardeners who want an earlier crop than can be had from seed. I'd rather grow my own, starting them in a hot frame in early December, keeping the rows two inches apart, sowing five or six seeds per inch. Keep the plants near the glass after they germinate to prevent excessive stem growth. When they get five inches tall, thin and transplant to stand an inch apart. Trim the tops to relieve transplanting strain. Some growers also cut the roots back to three-quarters of an inch. These techniques will produce a compact plant. After hardening off set them out two weeks before the last average frost date if the weather is good.

The second method is to plant sets, which are nothing more than tiny onion bulbs. Growers start them in spring, stop watering when they're pea- to marble-sized, lift the plants, sort and grade, and sell the next spring as sets. They will sprout and develop into regular onions by the end of summer. They're very cheap and convenient. The drawback is that mature onions from sets don't store as long as mature onions from seed, and you can't always get the variety you want. Still, if I had a small garden, lived in a northern climate, and wanted the most production I could get, I would consider growing plants from sets.

Last is growing directly from seed. The advantages are many. I have a choice of varieties. There's no transplanting shock. I can develop a homegrown strain by selecting the earliest maturing, largest onions with narrow necks. I have more control over growth, and I don't have to bother with nonorganic, chemically treated stock.

Much of what I know about growing onions comes from a pleasant encounter on a late spring day in Eureka. I was delivering newspapers—a job that gave me many opportunities to check the neighborhood gardens—when I came to a yard I hadn't noticed before. Behind the picket fence was a front yard filled with vegetables.

The side and the back yards were the same. I saw mostly garlics and onions, all of them remarkably vigorous and large. The owner, who was hoeing among them, noticed my interest and introduced himself. He was Grover Waldroop, a spry old gent who had been a gardener for most of his seventy-plus years. His specialty was garlics, which he sold to local natural food stores.

Grover insisted I come in, and as we walked among the vegetables, he gave me the first of several detailed accounts of how he grew super-quality alliums. I was so impressed that eventually I converted my own plantings to his strains and techniques. It would have been foolish not to. Grover has better than a half-century of observation and successful experience behind him.

The basis of his rich harvests is humus. "You can't grow a good crop without humus," is his unrelenting organic judgment. He processes most of the green matter that enriches his garden by composting it. He begins the season in September, as I do, using ground where I harvested field peas or favas that dried on the vines. "Garlic is easy to grow because it's a bulb," Grover says. "Onions are hard. They come up in a week when the weather's good but you have to have good eyes to tell them from the grass sprouts. Weeds'll run right over them. You have to weed as soon as you can. At my age it's hard work to grow onions from seeds. Too much close work and bending over. I'd rather grow garlic."

Grover has some very definite opinions on cultivation. "There's no worse onion than one grown in hard ground. You've got to cultivate to keep the soil loose around the bulbs. You take a man eating a big dinner. If his belt is loose he's going to eat a lot of food and not be uncomfortable. An onion or garlic is the same way. Give them lots of food and loose ground and they'll get big and fat."

Grover's not as big on mulches as I am. I apply a thick mulch in late fall to keep down weeds, and pull it back in March to add a compost band four inches wide and two inches deep down either side of the plants, working it into the soil as deep as possible without disturbing the roots. Grover and I are agreed on the next point, however. We break all flowering stalks when they appear. The reason? Grover sums it up, "Let an onion go to seed and you'll get a small bulb. You answer me, would you rather eat onions or onion seeds?"

The main thing I do from spring until August is keep the soil under the mulch from drying out. I stop watering, however, when the first plant matures and dies back. This gives the bulbs an opportunity to develop a tough, scaly protective outside as well as allowing the tops to dry out.

The crop I plant in March often goes into ground that was under mulch or a cover like rye or rape over winter. I grow more "keeper" than sweet onions at this sowing because fall-harvested bulbs last longer than those gathered in August. It's fine with me if any of the bulbs seem to be forming half above the surface as this gives them an easier way to expand. I simply draw mulch right up and over the exposed bulbs to keep them moist and growing.

Grover's harvest plan suits me fine. When two-thirds of the tops have died back he walks down the rows. "Here's one that's still growing. Stiff-necked. Just like some people. Too stubborn to know when to quit. Mark this now." He kicks it over, breaking the top. "When they don't know enough to die back, you encourage them," he says with a twinkle. Shortly thereafter they're ready to be pulled up and field-cured for a few sunny days. The properly cured plants have necks that appear shriveled with no sign of being plump or green. They should be stored in onion sacks (to provide good air circulation) in a cool, dry place. Grover sorts his. "Remember I told you to mark those thick necks. Eat them first. They won't last the winter. Use up the earliest ones first. The thin late ones will last the winter."

As far as varieties go, Crystal Wax, White, Yellow,

and Red Bermudas are excellent for raw fresh eating. My wife likes the whites for out-of-hand eating because of their mild, sweet flavor. None are particularly long keepers. My choice for keepers is the Minnesota Globe. It will stay solid longer than any other onion I know. The Southport Yellow and Red Globes are two other good keepers. I'm partial to the reds because I think they have more vitamins than the others.

One important point: always try to keep the onions moist. If the ground dries out the bulbs may split, in which case they'll be very poor keepers. Ample water and a thick mulch are the solutions to this problem.

Garlic Everything I said about onion culture is true about garlic. Garlics are grown for the cloves, which are natural divisions of the bulb. I plant them two inches deep, three inches apart, in rows twelve inches apart. There are three major choices: Italian red garlic which seems to have the strongest flavor, white silverskins which last longest in storage, and the giant or elephant garlic which has cloves big enough to be prepared as a vegetable in their own right. Never plant a whole bulb. Always select the biggest bulbs you can find for seed, and then take only the outermost circle of cloves, and plant them. By reselecting every year you'll soon have the biggest garlics in the neighborhood. To store, cut the stems like onions, or braid the whole dried plants into ropes and hang in a cool, dry place. Garlic will assist you in your battle against disease and pests if you plant it in a "here a clove, there a clove" way throughout the garden (except among the beans and peas which are antagonistic toward garlic).

Leeks Again, everything I said about onions applies to leeks too, except that they're not grown from bulbs. For the long-stemmed kind you'll need to blanch them, drawing up the soil around the base of the plant and the lower parts of the stem. (The result is no light hits these parts, and they turn from green to cream colored.) Either hill up the plants as you cultivate, or plant them in trenches and draw in the earth as they grow. Begin when they're half-grown and keep them buried to the juncture of the main leaves and stem. The blanching produces a milder flavor, but it doesn't do anything for the vitamin content of the plant. I make one planting in June. It will grow well into the autumn, but is usable anytime after it's six to eight inches tall. Leeks are hardy and will stand in good shape for months, going through rains and light frosts. In fact, the frost brings out the famous leek flavor and that's the reason they're best matured at the end of the season. As a vegetable or appetizer the blanched stalks are cut top and bottom and served cooked. American Flag, which has a stalk that is sometimes more than two inches in diameter, is the kind available from most seed stores. I also plant Italian Winter Leek because it grows even bigger. To grow big plants thin to stand three inches apart in rows fifteen inches apart.

Shallots Whenever I hear about shallots I think of some rare and mysterious gourmet food available only to the knowledgeable at premium prices. Actually, the shallot looks like a garlic without the outer skin that covers the bulb, and it's just as easy to grow. There's absolutely no reason why it's a rare and expensive vegetable for use only in the highest of haute cuisine. It has a very mild onionlike flavor, and its pointed, greyish cloves stand out a bit from the center of the bulb. Plant next to carrots in spring and you'll have a crop in fall, to be stored as you would garlic.

Chives This onion relative grows in clumps and, if not cut too much, sends up a very pretty purple rose flower. It's suitable for warm climates like the sunny windows of a kitchen or bathroom. I use it to flavor cottage cheese, eggs, and miso (soybean) soup. Seeds are available, but it's easier to find somebody who has a plant and get a start. You can grow chives in rows, as a permanent border, or just in clumps wherever you have space. Every few years divide the clumps to avoid overcrowding. Harvest by cutting off as many hollow leaves as you need with a sharp knife. In mild climates this crop will grow all winter, but elsewhere, unless you protect it, it will die back during a hard freeze.

Caring for Carrots

I once owned a plot of stony ground that was very well drained and conveniently close to a spring, but so poor that nothing grew on it, thanks to the work of a bulldozer during a logging operation. Because I liked the location I decided to transform it into a carrot bed. During one winter I removed about ten yards of stones that wouldn't pass through a quarter-inch mesh, leveled a small mound, terraced, and added leaf mold by the ton, well mixed into the top two feet of soil. I finished off by liming at the rate of ten pounds per 100 square feet to bring the moderately acid condition of the soil up to a minimum of pH 6. In the early spring I planted carrots, and by late June I was eating a delicious, well-shaped harvest.

I say all this for two reasons. First, if you have a practically worthless soil like I had, you can convert it into very productive gardening ground. You only have to do the hard work once. Second, stone-free earth is especially receptive to carrots and other root crops. Corn, beans, melons—most other crops—will do very well on well-developed stony ground, but carrots and other root crops are very touchy about running into stones as they grow. Sometimes they'll fork, other times they'll be misshapen, but mostly they won't develop their full size. Too much of their energy goes into fighting adverse conditions. So cater to the carrot's particular needs, even if you have to dig up your whole garden to do it.

If you are stuck with stony ground, a heavy clay soil, or a shallow hardpan condition (dirt that has formed itself into a cementlike layer), you can plant Oxheart or Guerande, which grows outward instead of downward. I've had good results with this variety in clay soils. Otherwise, the best early carrot is Touchon, a super-sweet strain of Nantes, which in itself is an excellent carrot. The roots are six to seven inches long and very deep orange and crisp. The difficulty with it is that it's strictly a first and second early-sowed crop. It won't develop its peak flavor in hot weather. The Coreless Nantes is another good medium-sized carrot that deserves a place in the early spring garden. From the time I leave off with Touchon until the beginning of August my main crop is a variety of Chanteney called Goldenheart or Burpee's Goldenheart. This is among the finest all-around carrots and will stand throughout the winter. I back it up with Half Long Danvers, a very heavy cropper with a rich orange color, fine grain, crisp taste, and very little core. It's probably the most-planted home and market carrot in America. Additionally there are excellent winter keepers like St. Valery and Imperator (both of them a little shy on flavor), and several very sweet midgets.

Carrots are hardy. It's possible to plant them two to four weeks before the average last frost date. The earlier date is safe if the winter has been mild and the long-range outlook is good. I'm a firm believer that gardeners should keep abreast of the weather, even to the point of jotting down conditions in their notebooks. Almanacs, the U.S. Weather Service long-range forecasts, and some magazines like state farm journals publish forecasts, which when taken altogether and added to your own observations, should give you an educated guess about planting time.

I plant in late February by sprouting seed indoors in a damp, rolled-up towel. As soon as the tiny roots appear I sow the seed a half-inch deep. This can save a week or more in germinating time. Later in the season I sow directly in the ground. I always prepare the ground deeply, as deep as my spade will go, although the soil doesn't necessarily have to be turned over to that full spade depth. In fact I think constantly bringing subsoil to the surface and putting topsoil six to eight inches deep is both unnatural and unnecessary on good ground. The point is to loosen up the soil so the roots will have an easy time penetrating and widening. I compost at the rate of a heaping shovelful per foot of row, well worked into the top inches, plus a sprinkling of rock phosphate, and I have plenty of natural and added potash at all times. If you don't have a rich supply of potash, apply wood ashes at the rate of two pounds for each twenty feet of row, or granite dust at twice that rate. Rake the seed bed smooth, set off rows at twelve inches, and plant.

As I mentioned in the lettuce chapter I like to plant companion carrots among the lettuce rows. That came about one day in a community garden in which I was involved. The husband of the schoolteacher I know was enthused about a new carrot scheme he had.

"Carrots take a lot of work to thin, right?" he asked.

"Right."

"But we all like carrots, right?"

"Right."

"That means we have a lot of work ahead of us?"

"Right."

"Wrong!" he exclaimed. "I've got a plan that will revolutionize carrot growing."

The revolution was that instead of crawling on my hands and knees to thin and weed one row at a time, I could now crawl on my hands and knees working two rows at once because he had planted closely spaced double rows. His ace-in-the-hole was not so much the saved labor, but the implications this system had for the whole garden. "When you make closely spaced rows you set up a micro-ecosystem," he explained. "You have better space utilization. You have companion planting that confounds bugs. The way I figured it out here is tremendous." He waved a piece of paper in front of my face.

The carrot diagram showed each carrot staggered on the diagonal with the carrots in the rows across from it. A first thinning called for plants left a half-inch apart. A second thinning came just as the roots began to touch. This left a final spacing in the diagram of two to two and a half inches between the carrots.

"The beauty of it is that you don't compact nearly as much soil while working. And the holes left by the ones you thin and eat when they're half-grown are perfect spaces for the ones that are left to grow into," he continued. "Now that I think about it, I bet we could just broadcast seed into a bed and then. . . ."

I didn't wait for the results of his new burst of reasoning and paperwork. My back was beginning to ache with the thought of thinning entire beds of carrots.

Regardless of how I plant I apply a light mulch after the seedlings emerge, and put on a deep mulch when the tops are six to seven inches. Often the crown will stick out of the soil and turn green. I don't know if this hurts the quality any as most people cut off the crown anyway. A thick mulch drawn right up around the plants solves the problem of green crowns.

Carrots always taste sweeter when they're about two-thirds to three-quarters grown, so besides eating the tender thinnings I make it a point to begin using carrots for the table before they're full grown. The exception is the winter crop which I always allow to mature, and pull when needed throughout the winter. The carrot is a crop that will store better in the ground than in a root cellar if you can prevent alternate freezes and thaws with a thick mulch. For this purpose clip the tops an inch above the crowns, cover with a dry mulch, and heap earth over that. I make my last planting in late July and it matures in November. Since growth is so imperceptibly slow after that date, and carrots stand well in the ground after maturity anyway, I don't clip tops or cover. That's the advantage of living in a climate where the ground doesn't freeze. My carrots retain their crispness up to the time they resume growth in spring.

For a small family planting, sow an initial ten feet of row, and follow that every two weeks with additional five- or ten-feet-long sections. Then in mid-July make a final planting as big as you can afford to make it, placing the carrots between brassicas if necessary. Cabbages and cauliflowers will crowd carrots in the end but the tops of the latter should rise high enough above the spreading leaves to fare well.

Beets and Chard

Crops that serve dual purposes give me a great deal of satisfaction. Two such crops are beets and chard. The beet is a green vegetable with leaves that contain more than 7,000 units of vitamin A per cup, cooked, plus respectable amounts of iron, calcium, riboflavin, and other vitamins and minerals. It is also a root crop with a delicious maroon or golden root. The chard is a greens crop (often called spinach beet) that produces from one spring almost to the next in my climate. Its double-duty advantage is that while it's producing a crop for you its root system is delving deep into the subsoil bringing up minerals that are out of the reach of most other crops, opening channels for the soil to breathe and drink, and adding humus to the

141

lower soil layers as it decays. The chard uses a lot of nutrients when the leaves are picked over a long season, but this drain is more than repaid by the improved physical structure of the soil for the next crop.

From what I can gather historically the plants we call beet and chard today are varieties of one leafy species known to the ancients. Apparently as gardeners cultivated the plant two distinct types arose so that by the late Middle Ages there was a beet grown for its roots and another for its greens. The root type further evolved in Central Europe into several types of the common beet. One has a maroon root, a second has a sweeter golden root and is more favored in Europe, a third is grown primarily for its greens and for bunching, and another is the sugar beet that provides a significant amount of the table sugar in the United States. Last there is the mangel, which some people believe is really a rutabaga. It grows to huge size and is a stock feed. All are available from gardeners' seed houses; their culture is pretty much the same, although spacings vary greatly.

The second variety of beet didn't develop an edible root, but its leaves grew to large size, closely bunched together, and with prominent, tender midribs. Gardeners began reselecting the seed until it turned into the Swiss chard. It's a major crop in my garden—one that I keep in production year-around.

To assure a continuous supply of these edible members of the goosefoot family I make my first beet planting in mid-February. They like cool, not cold, weather, and I get my best beets from these early sowings and from those that mature in the very late fall. Summer beets, while passable, tend to be a bit woody, and not as delicately flavored. I open a V-furrow about four inches deep and as wide, and fill it with compost. Then I add lime at the rate of a pound per twenty feet of row and mix it into the compost and topsoil. Beets respond marvelously to lime when used to bring acid soils to near-neutral pH. I don't know why this is so, although I do know it's not because they're large calcium users. Collards, for example, use twice as much calcium as beets based on an analysis of the amount in their ash, yet they will thrive in a soil 100 times more acid than beets like. After liming I work the dirt I had taken out of the furrow back in with the compost and usually end up with a slightly rounded planting bed.

The first time I planted I had so many seedlings I didn't know what to do with them all. The next year I resolved to sow only one seed per inch. I still got crowded seedlings. This continued for years until one day a group of us went on a nature hike around our Whale Gulch homes. The event sticks in my mind because afterwards we went over to Ray Raphael's house. Ray is the author of *An Everyday History of Somewhere*. Alicia Bay Laurel, herself the author of a couple of books in the "back to the land" tradition (how's that for down-home name-dropping?), washed and salt-rubbed our feet. While all this was going on it was perhaps one of Ray's botanist friends, up from Berkeley to enjoy the southern Humboldt scenery and help us key out useful wild plants, who mentioned that some seeds are properly not seeds at all, but fruits that contain many seeds, like beets.

"Like beets," echoed in my mind. No wonder I always got more seedlings than the number of seeds I planted. So now I'm resigned to the fact that when I take an ounce of seed and sow a fifty-foot row I'll end up with enough seedlings for a hundred feet. I find that presoaking to soften the corky seed capsule accelerates germination. I make the rows a foot apart, and thin the beets to stand two inches apart. A lot of commercial growers side-dress at the final thinning. It's true that beets taste best when they grow rapidly in cool weather on a loamy soil with plenty of moisture and nutrients. Yet for the first few years I never side-dressed any crop and all grew well. Later I moved into a period of side-dressing just about everything. Lately I've decided that while it's a beneficial practice for some crops, like leafy greens or radishes or those that will produce heavily over a long season, it's perhaps not so important with root crops in the organic garden. My advice is to experiment with side-dressing and not side-dressing at the same time. If the dressed beets show the same resistance to pests and disease as the others, are as crisp and flavorful in both root and leaf, but produce more of both, I say side-dress. If resistance to disease is lowered or the crop is less flavorful, don't side-dress. As a guide for beets the Rodale book, *How to Grow Vegetables and Fruits by the Organic Method,* advises that at the time you thin your beets for the last time, "a side-dressing of nitrogenous fertilizer—cottonseed meal or bloodmeal—may be applied at the rate of five pounds per 100 foot of row."

I suggest that small gardeners grow beets by making a sowing of five feet of row every two weeks right up to the first week of August. In the mild winter areas like southern California planting can continue into September. I find that if I get my last crop in toward the end of August I can expect a final harvest in December. The roots will remain in the ground in excellent condition for a couple months. If you have to lift your crop for storage, clip off all but the top one-fourth inch of greens and store in a very moist place. If the roots dry out any they'll get corky. Don't remove the final crop from the field before the ground starts to freeze as a few frosts will probably make the roots more flavorful. Gardeners who want to force beets will find it relatively easy to do, but it shouldn't be done until about February in really cold weather areas. If beets get too much cold weather in the middle of their lives they'll bolt to seed. To force beets sow in the hotbed and leave them there to mature. You can transplant them outdoors but my own experience with starting beets under glass in January and transplanting them to the field for an early harvest has convinced me that it's more work than it's worth. Field-grown beets come in nearly as early in my climate. I've found, too, that while the beet transplants, it doesn't always produce the same first-class roots as the field-sown root.

I plant two varieties for spring and summer use. Crosby's Egyptian is finely flavored and suited to cool weather in spring; Detroit Dark Red is the standard beet for roots and greens in the United States. The crop I sow in August for overwinter use is about half Detroit and half Winter Keeper. The latter is exactly what its name implies, and is probably the best choice for those who must store beets for long periods in root cellars.

I grow chard nearly the same way I do beets. One difference is that I make only two sowings—one in early spring for greens up to fall, and a second in August that will produce all winter. I find that the spring planting sends up seed stalks after several heavy pickings, and that while I can keep using the plants by breaking off the stalks, they're not really that productive by midsummer. I find it better to start with fresh plants for fall and winter production. I space the plants at six to seven inches in the rows that are fifteen inches apart. At the time of the final thinning I side-dress this crop with one pound of bloodmeal for every fifteen feet of row. Chard needs the extra boost because it will produce for about five or six months during a period when soil nitrogen-releasing bacteria are working at a greatly reduced rate. When the first leaves are ready to pick the plants will be about seven inches tall. It's possible to cut and use the whole plant at this time, but that's the end of the harvest. By picking the outer leaves on a regular basis, even if you compost or feed them to livestock, the plants will continue to develop fresh, tender growth, and you won't have any tough old leaves.

Through experimenting with every variety of chard I could find I've settled on Rhubarb for my red variety and Lucullus for my green. I believe the latter is better flavored, but the former probably has more vitamins because of its deeper color (it's red while the other's stalks are white). Fordhook Giant deserves mention for its size if nothing else. I use chard fresh in salads, in any dish calling for spinach or beet greens, in quiches, and in loaves. It's extremely prolific; fifteen feet of row in the spring and another fifteen feet for the fall will adequately supply a family of five.

10
The Brassicas

I still remember the astonishment I experienced the first winter I grew cabbages along the north coast. The taste was so sweet and delicate that I made whole meals out of December and January leaves, fresh from the garden, dipped in tahini and miso, a soybean and sesame seed mixture. There is absolutely no comparison between this delicious raw vegetable organically grown in a proper cool season and the common store-bought product.

In addition to cabbage, there are numerous other cultivated members of the mustard family. In fact, the vegetables included in the genus brassica are so numerous that I'm going to treat them under several groupings. First I'll discuss the general requirements for cabbage, cauliflower, broccoli, and brussels sprouts, and then I'll give specifics for each. Finally, I'll fill in on collards, kale, kohlrabi, turnips, and rutabagas.

I wish I could say cabbages (and here I include cauliflower, broccoli, and brussels sprouts as I'll do for the remainder of this general discussion) grew themselves, but that's not the case. Scores of diseases and pests attack them. The most notorious in my garden are the cabbage root maggot and the cabbage worm. You may also have trouble with clubroot, a fungus that causes yellowing, wilting, and misshapen and rotted roots, and possibly ends in death. Happily, the methods I use to grow the susceptible brassicas tend to minimize these problems.

Growing cabbage begins on ground that hasn't been planted to them in about five years. In a small garden this is not easy—and in fact may be impossible. I hold it up as an ideal. Cabbage is a very heavy feeder, and that's why I like to set out the late planting in land that has just undergone a year in a vetch-clover rotation. Clovers deposit a lot of nitrogen and leave the soil in a condition brassicas like. The earth should be well drained, toward the silt or clay loam side with plenty of humus for water retention, and with a pH between 6 and 6.8. As a general rule I add about ten pounds of dolomite, broadcast per 100 square feet of cabbage patch, worked into the top couple inches of soil. In addition to the nutrients already in the soil I dig a hole about twelve to fifteen inches deep, and nearly as wide, and fill it halfway with compost. I mix the dirt back into the hole so it is slightly mounded, and place a twig in the center as a marker. With this the field is ready for transplants.

The cabbage year begins in January. I set out plants in late February, but elsewhere you might have to start plants in February to set out from mid-March to the beginning of April. I sow seeds one inch apart in one-inch rows, covering with a quarter-inch of finely sifted soil. None of the brassicas benefit by too rich a potting medium (they get spindly), so I don't give them any liquid nutrient feeding except the day before setting in the field. When the plants are about three inches high I transplant them to other flats at four-inch intervals. This gives me a stockier plant, although I admit I often miss this intermediate transplanting and end up with a lot of crowded, long-stemmed plants. My practice of giving the plants cover but very little heat after they germinate helps minimize "legginess." When it does happen I bury the stems in the earth. If the soil is well drained and rich in humus, those portions of the stem underground will actually form roots, often boosting growth rather than holding it back.

In outlining my transplanting method for brassicas in this chapter, and for lettuces earlier, I've stressed the ideal way, but in a pinch these plants can take a lot. One afternoon I went to visit Peggy Etcheverry up on the Ettersburg Road. It was late July and she had a bunch of cabbages left over from an outdoor starter row.

"How you fixed for cabbages?" she asked.

At the time I was gardening a small plot and hadn't given any consideration to winter cole crops. I was going to plant roots and salad greens in the limited space I had. I told her I didn't have any cabbages.

"Well then, you've got to have some. They don't take up that much space." She grabbed a shovel and a cardboard box and dug seven or eight plants out of the row and dumped them in.

It was a couple of days before I got around to finding a place for them. I half hoped they would die, and then I wouldn't be bothered (it's hard not to replant something if it's still alive). Meanwhile they remained in a crumbly earth ball in a box next to the compost heap. In setting them out most of the dirt fell off the roots and some of the leaves were broken. I didn't expect much from them, but that December and January they produced some of the biggest, sweetest heads I've ever eaten. As I said, they can take it.

Assuming you are going to handle your cabbages with a little more care, an important step is to dust the root ball and stems with wood ashes. After I firm the plant into its permanent home I sprinkle ashes all around the plant to a distance of three or four inches to help repel maggots. Each time I cultivate (except at the first cultivation which is just a few days after transplanting) I apply more ashes to control weeds. After the plants have been in the soil a month and a half I side-dress with a handful of a fifty-fifty mixture of compost and bloodmeal in a circular band three inches deep and six inches out from the stem. At this point I also dig carefully around the juncture of root and stem to see if there's maggot activity. If there is I mix ashes fifty-fifty with rotenone and apply to a depth of one inch around the plants as well as dust the lower portions of the stem and leaves. If cabbage butterflies are around I dust the entire plants with the mix, and look on the underside of leaves for eggs which I then destroy.

The first season after I moved to the Lighthouse Ranch from the south part of Humboldt County I found out just how diligent I had to be in this search. I was sitting in the garden office one afternoon going over planting records when my assistant, Paul LaMontaigne, came in and wanted to know what was the matter with the cabbages.

"Nothing's the matter with the cabbages," I replied. We had about 300 plants out that were just beginning to head up nicely. I had walked through the rows on my rounds that morning and they looked fine.

"All I know is they look like they're dying," Paul insisted.

We went out to the cabbage patch and sure enough, scattered throughout the rows were plants that were fallen over dead, or were at a dangerous degree of wilting. I was astonished. A plant near me showed signs of wilt and as I moved it to examine it, it broke off in my hand.

"Hey, look at this!" Paul exclaimed.

There were small white maggots around the severed root. It was a heartbreaking experience, especially because we couldn't do much about it at that point, although it did teach me to give my crops more than a visual check. Often maggot activity won't be apparent until the plant suddenly falls over dead, the stem severed from the roots. Since that first bad experience I've used chickens to good advantage in maggot and worm control, but haven't always been successful in keeping either the birds or the bugs from tender young plants.

Some old-time growers used to cultivate very deeply around their brassicas on the assumption that the root systems would be forced to go very deep. They would then pick up all kinds of extra nutrients and plenty of water. I believe this is a good practice in certain

150

instances as I've mentioned elsewhere, but because I mulch all brassicas heavily, deep cultivation isn't possible after I side-dress. By way of compromise I encourage deep root growth by making my compost holes deep and by allowing the top half-inch of soil to dry out before irrigating. My main mulch goes on after I side-dress unless a catch crop is still in the rows—if so, I wait until it's harvested. Six inches of seaweed is my favorite mulch.

The catch crop is usually leaf lettuce or some other greens because they vacate the space before brassicas need it. I also find it convenient to plant garlic every few feet for pest protection.

For my winter crop I replant all the same varieties again in outdoor nursery rows, sowing half in early June and half in early July. Transplants are ready in a month to six weeks after sowing.

Broccoli

The two varieties I plant are DiCicco (forty-eight days), a green sprouting type, and Calabrese (fifty-eight days). Just about every seed rack has one or the other of these two. The other common sort, Neptune Hybrid, usually costs more per packet and doesn't seem to do as well for fall harvests. I transplant to eleven by eighteen inches, and harvest the terminal head just as soon as it looks like it won't gain any more size. I pick the side shoots as they appear. As with cauliflower, I don't let them rice. By giving the plants manure or fish emulsion feeding just when I cut the first head the plants will continue to bear side shoots, some of them quite large, for several months. My fall crop produces all winter by this method.

Brussels Sprouts

This crop is well suited for my climate. I plant in June and harvest from October to spring. Frost enhances the flavor. In cold areas it will bear until the first killing frost, and should be given protection before then, as outlined for cabbages in cold frames. The lower buttons, or sprouts, mature first and when I see them starting to form I break off the lower leaves to allow space and energy to go into sprout production. I leave a leafy top. I imagine that the plants look like some strange, small palm tree. In central coastal California the commercial growers pinch out the leafy crowns when the buttons form. They claim this makes extra big sprouts. I don't have the heart to do this. It makes the plants look too forlorn. There is not much of a variety to choose from. Long Island Improved is the standard, but there's also Jade Cross Hybrid for home plantings. Either will produce up to 100 buttons under optimum conditions.

Cabbages

I sow cabbages a half-inch deep in nursery rows and transplant to stand two by two feet in the rows. Sometimes this is too close, so I harvest the immature heads of some to make rooms for others. To determine ripeness press the head—when it feels hard to the touch, it's ready. Before that it has "give." The hands-down best early variety of cabbage is Jersey Wakefield. Generally speaking no variety but this one achieves its best flavor under warming conditions. That's why fall crops taste better. I back Jersey with All Head Early which matures in 78 days to the former's 62. I sometimes plant Red Acre instead. It's a nicely flavored, maroon variety. Next comes Early Flat Dutch and Danish Ball Head, 85 and 100 days to maturity, respectively so that from one sowing I have several months' worth of harvests. For the family garden I suggest growing Jersey Wakefields in 10-day successions. The heads are compact, and usually not over three pounds. For the fall crop my main variety is Stonehead, a wilt-resistant type that takes 110 days to mature, but which will stand storage better than any other I know. I back this up with more Red Acre and Early Flat Dutch.

An old-timer up Gibson Creek in Whitehorn has a good way of keeping plants in the field after they mature. I came by one autumn morning thinking to chitchat about woolly bear caterpillars and other weather indicators. He was out in the garden digging around his cabbages with a spading fork.

"What's up?" I asked.

"You got eyes." It was his way of telling me if I watched what he was doing I'd get the picture without asking silly questions.

"You're digging cabbages," I offered.

"Nope."

"You're cultivating."

"Nope."

I could see he was getting a chuckle out of my greenhorn answers. "OK, you tell me."

"Watch." He pushed the spading fork the length of the tines into the ground about ten inches from the plant and made as if to lift the plant—roots and all—out of the earth. He repeated the process on the other side of the cabbage. "You see that?"

I nodded.

"You get it?"

I shook my head in the negative.

He spit out some juice from his tobacco chaw. "This

here digging and pulling breaks the roots. They don't grow no more—least ways they don't grow much. When it rains the heads don't split. You can keep them right here in the ground a long time."

"How long?"

"Couple, three, four months. How do I know? I eat them before *that*."

Another method I've heard about but never tried because of the mildness of my climate is to lift the plants out and put them in the dirt of a cold frame that's been kept from freezing. This is like a giant transplant operation. I harvest by cutting the stem right beneath the head. This leaves the coarse lower leaves on the roots. If I didn't lift the roots (unnecessary when plants aren't going to stand a long time in the field) the plants will regenerate cabbage-ettes. Sometimes I feed the leaves to livestock (the cows only get as much as they'll eat in about an hour after morning milking—too many complaints about off-flavor otherwise). Eighty plants is more than enough for an average family in a year, and you should get that many transplants from one packet.

Cauliflower

I grow two crops of cauliflower—one in January and one in June. I set them eighteen inches apart in rows twenty-four inches apart. In the nursery rows I sow a half-inch deep, an inch apart, and thin to four inches in all directions. I prefer the self-blanching sorts, but sometimes I still have to tie the top leaves over the curd (head) to get that creamy appearance and tender flavor. The time to do it is just when the heads start to form, while the plants are dry, but just after a deep irrigation. Check in a week and they should be about ready. I harvest all cauliflower before the heads start to "rice," or lost their tightness. (Once you see it happen you'll know what I'm talking about.) I plant Super Snowball (fifty-five days) and Super Danamerica (sixty-six days). A packet of seed is enough for the average gardener who sows transplants an inch apart by hand in the flats or nursery.

Collards

Collards is a greens crop and thrives in hot weather. I keep my plants alive and producing year-around by making a spring sowing and a fall sowing, and by picking only the outer leaves. Space the plants to stand twelve inches apart in rows eighteen inches apart for the variety Vates. The Georgia strains might need more room as they grow very tall and bushy. Frost improves flavor. Unless you're a collards lover, one or two plants for variety's sake will be all you want.

Kale

Kale is one of my favorite vegetables. It's very high in vitamins A and C, and a tremendous producer of greens year-around. I make my major planting in late July, sowing seed an inch apart in rows fifteen inches apart. I thin to stand nine to twelve inches in the rows. It's important to pick the outer leaves whether or not you'll eat them, to encourage new growth and to keep the inner leaves from getting tough. Kale stands heavy frosts, and where the ground doesn't freeze too much, you could probably keep it producing in an insulated cold frame most of the winter. In mild climates it will grow all winter. I eat it raw or cooked. After trying every variety I could find I've settled on Dwarf Blue Curled Scotch and Blue Siberian. These are both reliable and well flavored. Frost improves their quality. A packet of seed is three or four times more than the average family needs, but it will store for three to five years under cool, dry conditions.

Kohlrabi

 Kohlrabi is a vegetable I grow because my father likes it, and his father probably liked it before him. No one anywhere, ever, has served me kohlrabi. I'm the only person I know who grows it, yet I see seed packets in the stores every year. The edible portion is the aboveground bulbous stem that tastes best when it's about an inch and a half to two inches in diameter. The flavor is delicately cabbagelike, but the consistency is firm and crisp like the crispest carrot you ever ate. I peel and eat kohlrabi raw like an apple.

Culture is easy. The best way is to plant in July so they'll mature in the cooler months of the year. Hot weather makes them tough and strong-flavored. I interplant with late beets, which make good companions. Make the rows twelve to fifteen inches apart. Seed should be a half-inch deep, thinned to stand six inches in the rows. Standard varieties are White Vienna and Purple Vienna, both of which also yield edible foliage, making them a good choice for the small garden where space is at a premium.

Turnips and Rutabagas: Getting to the Root of the Brassicas

As long ago as antiquity, European farmers began cultivating a wild cabbage, *brassica campestris*, for its edible root. By the time Hannibal crossed the Alps on his way to Rome the cultivated plant was much different than its uncultivated brother—so much so that had there been botanists at that time they might have classified it as a distant variety, *rapa*. Much later, some gardener in the Dark Ages, by chance or design, took that vegetable and crossed it with its relative, *b. napus*, the common rape I've mentioned as a cover crop, and ended up with still another vegetable, *b. napus*, var. *napobrassica*. Today in a multitude of varieties, some grown for their foliage and some for their roots, we grow these vegetables under the names turnips (early derived from the wild cabbage) and rutabaga (the possible turnip-rape cross).

Both are cool weather crops, reaching their peak development and flavor in the short, cool days of late fall and spring. Because of my particularly cool climate I can grow turnips year-around with very good results. Where summers are hot turnips tend to develop thick skins, get woody, and have a strong, undesirable odor. I only grow rutabagas to mature in fall, because those that go through a few light frosts are sweeter and more flavorful than those harvested before frost.

I grow turnips as fast as possible. This is the only way to develop a crisp, mild root. I sow them broadcast and in rows. I never thought of the former method until I visited Howard Orem just outside of Whitethorn. He was a newcomer to the area, but he had the fanciest organic spread for miles around. After he finished showing me the grounds he asked if I wanted any turnips because he had plenty. A whole field of plenty, it turned out. He had prepared a bed, sowed sparingly, and waited. Many of the roots were runts, but many were giants. Orem explained both turnips and rutabagas limit the size of their growth by the space allotted them. "It's really something," he said. "They'll fill up practically every square inch of ground. If you pick them at random while there's still growing temperature the ones that are left will expand into the vacated space."

I feel broadcast is best for winter storage crops or for those that will be fed to livestock. However, row planting seems to make for a milder vegetable in most circumstances. I figure a half-ounce of seed per 100 feet, in rows spaced twelve inches apart. A sandy loam is best, but any soil that you can stir up early in the spring and that is loose and friable will suffice. Turnips are not big nutrient users so it's not necessary to fertilize an organic soil in good condition. Save your composts and manures for the crops that follow turnips in the same rows. The two keys to certain, quick, mild turnips are frequent, shallow cultivation and timely thinning. Cultivate for weeds about four days after the crop is up and again at ten-day intervals, or when you thin. Thinning should be to two inches apart when the plants are an inch high and to three to six inches when they're six inches high. Thinnings—roots or greens—make good eating.

Among the different varieties the earliest of all is Extra Early White Ball, which matures in twenty-five to thirty days. It has a small root and will stand a three-inch spacing. So will Jersey Lily, a white variety that takes forty days. Like the early crops of most vegetables they're not as large and don't have quite the flavor of the main crop types, but I find them useful for getting newly grown crops other than radishes on the table in early spring. The standard main crop is Purple Top White Globe, a very dependable root for all seasons.

The Brassicas

There are also some greens types. I've planted Shogoin often in the past because it yields tender greens over a long period before bolting. Since it provides small roots as well it's especially suited to the gardener who has only a small area and wants to make maximum use of it. The vegetables known as broccoli raab, strap-leafed turnips, and seven-top all fall into this "leafy" class. The greens from the root turnips are only good at a very young stage. They get tough and prickly after the final thinning.

To keep the roots from getting tough I mulch just after the last thinning, keep the soil moist, and harvest any time after the roots are big enough to eat. They won't remain at their peak of tenderness for very long except in winter, so I prefer small succession plantings up to May 1. I pick up again in September with one crop for overwinter use.

The rutabaga is a much bigger vegetable than the turnip, and I think preferable for winter use. It tastes sweeter, has a firmer flesh, and a higher nutritional value. It's also hardier and remains in good shape longer when mature. Slow growth doesn't impair its quality if it's grown as a winter crop. The most-planted variety— American Purple Top—takes about ninety days to reach full maturity.

I sow them to stand six to eight inches in the rows that are fifteen inches apart. About one-quarter-ounce of seed, at the rate of one to the inch, will sow 100 feet of row, which is about four times more than the average family needs. While they thrive in any kind of soil in which turnips grow, they appreciate an even richer one. I like to follow a pea crop with rutabagas. There are two times to plant—between June 15 and July 1 for stock, and in mid-July for human consumption. For table use I follow the same cultural practices as for turnips. They stand hard rains and even frequent frosts if not severe, and will keep in good condition through the winter months where the ground doesn't freeze. I keep my rutabagas in rotation so that no member of the cabbage family occupies the same space for four years at least. If you find this impossible, try to give each section of your garden a rest from the brassica vegetables at least every other year.

11
Minor
Cool Weather Crops

There comes a point in gardening—if not in the planning, then in the planting—where you have to draw a line and say, "This vegetable, but not this one." In some instances it's a matter of taste; in others, a matter of space; and in still others, a matter of need. For example, do I really like endive (no), do I have room to grow dock or *gobo* (not really, considering all the other roots I grow), do I really need fennel (everytime I plant it I never use it). So with this in mind I present a very abbreviated list of the cool weather vegetables I plant from time to time, which either aren't very important to me or else aren't very important to others. The ordinary radish, for example, is not very important to me though I must admit I can't remember a year when I didn't grow at least one variety. The Jerusalem artichoke, on the other hand, is extremely important to me. It's the first market crop I ever sold and it yields prolifically in my environment. Other people might go their whole lives without ever having the inclination to eat one.

Minor Greens

The group I call the minor greens is really very versatile. It includes everything from cress, parsley, and coriander, which can be used as salad vegetables, to fennel, which has leaves that can be brewed into a tea. Several of the minor greens like chervil, parsley, and coriander are grown like carrots while cress and endive are cultivated more like lettuce. You might want to experiment with a small batch of each of these since they all have their own set of growing conditions and their own particular uses.

***

Chervil A member of the carrot family, chervil is quite easy to grow. I use its leaves like parsley. It has a slightly licorice flavor and goes well with seafoods. Grow it like carrots, and for continuous use, make successive sowings.

***

Cress There are three varieties of cress: upland, garden, and water. The first two grow on dry land, the third needs running water to develop to its full potential. Plant the way you would lettuce. Thin to stand three inches in the rows. Use them when they are young and tender for the pungent, hot flavor they add to salads. Water cress is a veritable mine of minerals. I used to harvest it as a market crop, putting it up in bunches. It grows from seed or from stem cuttings, and is easily transplanted to streams and brooks.

***

Endive This is a relative of chicory that grows like lettuce. The main difference between it and the latter is that it will stand hot weather. To produce a crisp salad vegetable you have to blanch the heart to remove the bitter taste. If the plant is too moist when you tie the larger leaves over the heart it could rot. Some people think endive is a gourmet treat.

***

Fennel The leaves make a nice tea and the bulbous part of the stalk can be eaten as a cooked vegetable. It's very hardy and grows wild in my area. It does take up a lot of space.

Mustard

Mustard This is one of my major minor crops. I grow it in early spring and late fall and handle it exactly like leaf lettuce. The leaves get too hot and bitter to eat in the summer and the plants are quick to bolt in hot spells. The variety called Mustard Spinach is among the best. I also grow Ostrich Plume and Florida Broad Leaf. The curly types are harder to clean of grit than the smooth-leaved ones. Mustard is high in vitamins.

Parsley and Coriander

Parsley and Coriander Culture for both of these is similar to carrots, the family to which they belong. Thin to stand three inches apart. Sometimes I never get around to thinning and they still do well. Parsley seed is slow to germinate, so I sow them with radishes the same way I sow radishes and parsnips together. Parsley transplants very well, but coriander doesn't. Make an early planting for summer use and an August planting for winter use. In cold winter areas transplant parsley to a hot frame or windowsill pot. I like Champion Moss Curled and the old-fashioned Giant Italian, a straight-leafed variety with a very pronounced parsley flavor that makes it ideal for drying. Of the rooted types I like Hamburg, which also provides greens. Coriander can be grown for seeds or leaves. Mexicans use it in salads, fruits, and in meat dishes under the name *cilantro*, a practice I heartily recommend.

Sorrel

Sorrel Two unrelated species, redwood sorrel and sheep sorrel, grow in abundance around our place, but I got a notion to have some garden sorrel so I planted

Mammoth Lyon, a perennial that does quite well in cool climates. One plant provides me with all the leaves I'll ever want.

Minor Roots

The minor roots consist of: Jerusalem artichokes, which are abundant growers; dock, a weed-like plant; celery and celeriac, long-season vegetables; and radishes, which have to be grown quickly so they don't get too hot. As with the minor greens, there is a wide variety among the minor roots. While I grow and eat a lot of Jerusalem artichokes, for instance, I very rarely grow dock. Radishes, on the other hand, are not only good for eating, but also can be used as protection against unwanted pests.

Celery and Celeriac These are long-season crops that have to be started early in cold weather areas. In California I plant them in June and harvest them in the fall and winter. I start in flats for better germination control, and transplant to the field when the plants are about three inches high. With plenty of water applied to the plants before, during, and after transplanting I've gotten nearly 100 percent "take" despite hot weather. Germinating seed, whether in the open or in flats, is much easier if you keep them under damp burlap until they break the surface. When the plants are four inches high cut the tops and this will make them compact. I make the rows two feet apart, and keep the plants six inches apart. Mulch deeply and keep drawing the mulch around the stems as the plants grow. Do this even with the self-blanching types, otherwise they develop a bitter taste. Celeriac doesn't have to be blanched because you want the root, not the greens. The basis of good celery is a continuous supply of water. The plants will stand frosts.

Dock This is a relative of the sorrel. It's available from some seed houses and is used in Japanese cookery under the name *gobo*. I've planted it for fun. It grows like a weed, and in fact is not far removed from that common weed, the giant burdock, which incidentally can be used for the same purposes the first year of its growth.

Jerusalem Artichoke This plant is a member of the sunflower family and will grow to a height of eight to ten feet in good soil. The edible portion is the tuber, which is something like a potato, but sugary rather than starchy. It's a very prolific yielder and will remain in excellent shape in the ground over winter if you apply a thick mulch.

I plant seeds twelve by twelve inches and about three inches deep. The ground should have a three-inch layer of compost dug into the surface. When the plants are a foot high I sprinkle a third each of bloodmeal, wood ashes, and rock phosphate at the rate of two pounds per 100 square feet. I then mulch and water. When the stalks die back in the fall, I trim them to a foot high to mark the locations of the tubers, to make digging easier, and to let the tops begin to break down. Some folks space two to four times as far apart as I do, but I find with a rich soil and water, the plants will yield quite well at the closer spacing.

The Jerusalem artichoke is a native vegetable that the Indians cultivated long before the Europeans arrived. It will grow just about anywhere, and isn't bothered at all by bugs in my garden. You divide the

165

tubers into "eyes" just like potatoes, and let them heal, again as you would potatoes. Plant anytime after it's warm enough to plant potatoes, though I rarely set mine out before late April. They will remain in the same spot for about four months so it's best to put them in an out-of-the-way north corner of the garden next to sunflowers or other tall growers. There are two strains— the French and the American. The first is very gnarled and has nooks and crannies where dirt accumulates and refuses to be cleaned out. The American tubers are smooth and potatolike. If you have the French strain, get rid of it; it's not worth the trouble to plant.

Radish   The successful radish grows on moist, loose soil well supplied with organic matter. Radishes have to grow fast or they get hot. They have to be harvested on time or they'll quickly get pithy, then woody and go to seed. Follow the directions on the seed packet. I never put radishes in any particular spot but pop a few feet in wherever I find space, especially between crops that haven't grown up enough to use all the space allotted to them. I also grow them between cabbages where root maggots are a problem. The idea is that the radishes will grow quickly and the flies will be attracted to them instead of the cabbages or other cole crops. The flies lay eggs on the radishes, the maggots emerge, and you pick and destroy the radishes and maggots, thus breaking up the fly life cycle and protecting your main crop.

My favorite varieties are Cherry Belle, French Breakfast, and White Icicle. In another chapter I'll discuss winter radishes because they have a different set of requirements than the smaller ones. All radishes do best in cool weather. In hot weather plant in shade. I've harvested delicious, mild roots in 100° weather by planting on the north side of a building.

166

12
Cool Weather Perennials

The ideal in organic gardening as I practice it is to emulate the principles nature employs to enrich the fertility of the earth. This is the reason I delight in perennial crops. Although men have devised techniques to maintain the fertility of the soil under artificial conditions of high productivity, nature allows certain crops to occupy the same space for years. We are not required to constantly plow and cultivate them, growing them first here and then there. Barring cataclysmic events such as floods, great pestilence, or fire, this vegetation becomes dominant and remains that way. I've heard of asparagus beds that were producing as well fifty years later as they did in their first years of production.

The perennials I'm going to talk about here have many needs in common. They require a portion of the garden all to themselves where they won't disturb or be disturbed by normal garden activities. They require very rich soils for optimum production, ample moisture during the period preceding and during their harvest seasons, deep mulches, abundant nutrients, and loving care to keep them free from competitive weeds and occasional pests. They also need to be thinned or replanted from time to time.

Asparagus

Asparagus is a relatively easy crop to grow, and once established, will stand a good deal of abuse and neglect from people and the elements. However, the way to fat, one-inch spears is not neglect, but care. The way I'll put my next bed in is the way veteran apple picker, Chauncey O'Shaunessey, told me out near Bridgeport, Washington.

"This is asparagus country," Chauncey told me. "Look around. It grows wild everywhere." In fact, we saw the fernlike branches of asparagus, covered with berries right in the middle of the empty lot where we were standing. That was autumn, months past harvest, so I didn't think much about asparagus after that. But when spring rolled around I was back in Bridgeport again, having a man with a tractor plow up two big garden plots for me. Just as he finished Chauncey stopped by.

"Did you see all the wild asparagus that guy dug up? They're tougher'n all get out," he said. "Saw a wild patch stop a tractor once in an orchard the other side of Okanogan." He paused to see if I was impressed (I was) and continued, "What you going to do with all those roots?"

I said, "Nothing. Throw them in the compost."

"How come?"

"We're only going to be here a season and there's plenty of wild asparagus to pick."

"It's a shame to see them go to waste. They cost a lot of money in the store. You could plant those heavy roots and have a dandy bed."

He didn't change my mind about composting them, but I was curious about how he would start a bed.

"In the old days," Chauncey said, "folks used to dig a trench a couple feet deep and pack it with manure before planting. I don't go for that. I dig a trench a foot deep and fill it halfway with manure. Then I take and toss in some dirt and put my roots in." He showed me how easy it was to spread out the roots from the crown like the spokes of a wheel. "Last you mix up half dirt and half old manure and cover the roots. And that's it."

"I heard you're supposed to leave them lower in a trench and draw soil over them as the sprouts grow," I said.

"I guess you could if you like fooling around after you're done with it, but my way's best. If anybody tells you different, they've done their asparagus-growing from an armchair."

The only observations I'd like to add about Chauncey's plan is that when the shoots reach surface level, sprinkle a cup of the following mixture: two-fifth bloodmeal, two-fifth rock phosphate, and one-fifth wood ashes over the topsoil for every three plants, gently working it in. I'd also prefer to use 100 percent compost in the trench instead of manure and dirt.

When the shoots are six inches high I mulch the plot, and maintain a minimum four inches of seaweed. The only time I draw away the cover is in late winter when I move away the mulch from part of the plot so it will warm and the asparagus will send up shoots about ten days earlier than in the mulched section. Conversely, the mulched section will produce ten days later, so I extend my season about three weeks through this method.

Now I want to backtrack some. You can establish an asparagus bed in two ways—by seed or buying one- or two-year-old roots. I advise not to buy two-year plants as they cost more and don't stand transplanting that well. Year-old roots are inexpensive, they're alive, and they'll bear a year ahead of seed. The last time I purchased roots they cost $7.50 per 100 compared to 80¢ an ounce for seed that has the potential to produce 1,000 plants. There's a question of economics. I'd say the home gardener who's not going to plant more than 100 plants will reap a dollar value greater by far with the started roots than if he started with seed. I think of this in terms of labor expended, and of the value of the vegetable.

The main varieties are Washington strains. I choose Mary Washington because it holds a tight bud a long time and is a large-stalked, rust-resisting plant. If you want to sow seed, do it in the spring in a well-prepared bed that has received a two-inch layer of compost. Make the rows two feet apart, presoak, sow sparingly, and thin to three inches in the row after they're up. Asparagus plants are very tiny and feathery at first and are easily overrun by weeds, so be diligent and careful when you cultivate.

The second year transplant them to their permanent beds as I described above. Whichever method you choose—roots or seed—space the plants to stand twenty inches apart in rows three feet apart. Don't harvest any spears that year or the next year. The roots will bear much more heavily and the stalks will be bigger if you wait. When you do begin harvesting wait until about four to six inches of stalk are showing and cut just below the ground level with a sharp knife, being careful not to damage the stalks that are getting ready to push through the surface. The mulch will keep the newly emerged stalks in beautiful shape until you harvest. After you've cut stalks for a month, it's time to quit so that the remaining stalks will turn into branches that provide for the next year's crop. Every spring add a two-inch layer of compost to the bed, which when incorporated with the mulch, will make a very loose soil so that earthworms and tiny soil creatures can do their valuable work.

The one problem you may have is the asparagus beetle, which will ruin a planting if not controlled. The easy solution is to let chickens or guinea hens scratch around in the patch. If you arrange your perennials so that they are all in one easily enclosed place you won't run the danger of the fowl causing damage in the garden.

Globe Artichokes

The artichoke isn't for everyone. It only grows well in a few places and not everybody appreciates it where it does grow. I admit to taking great enjoyment in sitting around the dining room table with friends, dipping leaf after leaf in melted butter, part with mayonnaise, and part with lemon and salt. Now you know one reason why I like artichokes.

The other reason is that the crop bears in late winter and early spring when there just aren't any fresh vegetables around except roots and greens. I'm not familiar with artichoke culture outside California, but as I understand it the plants must be protected from frosts by being cut back to about six inches. They should be put under a bushel, the bushel should be covered with a layer of dirt, and that with a one-foot layer of fresh manure for best results.

While it's possible to grow from seed started in flats or directly in the outdoor rows, the easier method of propagation is to remove suckers from parent plants. Plant the suckers four feet by four feet and six inches deep. Since artichokes peak out after about four years, the ideal plan I've developed is to divide the bed into five parts. One section has year-old plants; the next, two-year old, and so on. Each fall I take the suckers from the four-year plants and put them into a new section. At the end of the season I remove all the four-year olds and give the ground a cover crop. The cover stays on that season and the next season until late summer when I turn it under for another planting of artichokes. I think they could stay in the same area of the garden indefinitely as long as generous helpings of compost and much were applied and they didn't fall prey to any harmful disease.

The major consideration with artichokes is to keep them moist and well fed. Besides caring for them as I described for asparagus, it's good to give them a half-cup of the fertilizer I described for starting asparagus in September, if they're going to produce in the winter months. (see page 169) Cut off the head before the scales start to spread and use immediately. They start to get tough after reaching full size. Cut out the stalks that bore the heads and use them in the mulch or compost. I like my artichokes with about an inch or two of stalk left on as a handle. For variety, try them stuffed with mushrooms, parsley, bread crumbs, olives, and wheat germ.

Rhubarb

I'm going to be very succinct about this crop. Like the asparagus it prefers a region where there's a pronounced cold spell. This apparently gives the plant a recuperative rest from production. I give it the same treatment as I do asparagus. To plant I dig a hole about twelve to fifteen inches deep, fill it with compost within five inches of the top, set in a year-old crown, and cover with soil. Plants should be three feet apart in rows four feet apart. Supply abundant moisture. Confine your picking to a month or six weeks in spring, taking only well-developed outer leaves with heavy stalks. Because of the cool, moist climate along the north coast I make two harvests a year, one in mid-spring and another in late fall. The plants grow almost year-around. I give them an early fall feeding of a half-cup of the starter food I described for asparagus. (see page 169)

The way to harvest is to grasp a stalk in your hand, slide a thumb down the inner groove as far as it will go, then twist the stalk to the side and pull up. The stalk should come off without tearing or ripping off baby leaves. I snap off the inedible leaves and add them to the mulch around the plants. I also cut down all seed stalks as they take growing power away from the stalks. In good soil you'll find that every few years the crowns are getting crowded and the size of the stalks getting smaller. Then it's time to transplant. Do it in the fall so the plants will get an immediate start in their new home, or if you don't want additional rhubarb plants, you can take the roots and crowns and "plant" them in wooden boxes filled with dirt. Subject them to freezing temperatures for a month and bring them indoors where they will send up stalks until they're exhausted.

Cool Weather Perennials

There are two ways to divide the crowns. One is to dig up the whole plant and cut the crowns with sections of root, and replant. If a patch is in really bad shape I recommend this "starting over" procedure. If the plants are in good shape I allow the ground to dry out some, and then dig away the dirt around the crown to a depth of about four or five inches. With a sharp spade I split the crowns and roots, digging out half of the system for replanting or forcing.

There are several varieties available from root or seed. The seed, however, is not always exactly like the parent stock. Most-planted varieties include Cherry, MacDonald's Canadian Red, and Victoria. I have no idea what kind I have, but I know it's a heavy bearer of good quality fruit. After all that's the best criterion, so don't hesitate to take your neighbor's unnamed stock if it's good.

13
Warm Weather Crops

One year I decided to grow okra along the edge of the fog zone where I lived in northern Mendocino County. I got a packet of Clemson Spineless seeds and sowed them directly into the ground in May. In a few weeks little okra plants were growing up on the south edge of a small terraced plot. After a time the first ones flowered. And what beautiful flowers. I was extremely pleased. Then the blossoms dropped and I waited for the pods, but none appeared. Meanwhile flowers came and went, but I never harvested an edible pod. The reason: not enough heat.

Heat—when it comes, how long it stays, its intensity, its extremes, and its total amount—determines to a great extent the success of any crop, but it especially makes a difference with those we call the warm weather crops. While there may have been enough total heat over the frost-free growing season in my area for the okras, there was never an intense enough heat to give the flowers the opportunity to set fruit. Okras simply don't produce when the monthly average temperature falls below 65°.

Since common vegetables, with few exceptions, don't grow until the temperature reaches 40°, the last expected frost date will determine how early you can set out the early crops like lettuce, spinach, and peas. Similarly, the first expected frost date in the fall will determine how late you can grow unprotected warm weather vegetables. The time between the two determines whether or not certain vegetables will even mature. Chayote, for example, is a crop that needs both heat and time to ripen. You could have enough total heat to mature a chayote fruit, but if a frost comes before the required time has passed there won't be any crop. On the other hand, as soon as the temperature moves past a monthly average of 75°, mustard, spinach, and many other crops bolt to seed.

The average temperature of the month is an important factor in growing. This is simply the average high and the average low for the month added together and divided by two. Another important measurement is the number of growth degrees on any given day. To arrive at this number add the maximum and minimum temperatures for the day and divide by two. Subtract forty from that number and that's the growing temperature for that day. Most of this information—along with frost-date probabilities and rainfall data—is available either from local weather stations or the state agricultural extension service. The important point is to understand its application in the garden.

Working with the Heat Factor

No matter whether you grow your crops indoors, outdoors, or both, the temperature is the greatest variable, and subject to the least control. But the gardener who understands how to work within the heat factor will be the one who is very successful with the crops he grows.

For instance, the gardener who knows that growing crops out of season taxes the plants' resources and makes them more open to disease and pest attack carefully watches over his crops. Or, by taking advantage of certain ranges of temperatures, he knows he can plant and harvest some crops that would be subject to heavy insect attack if they were grown in normal seasons. Flavor and quality can be seriously impaired by too much heat or not enough. I used to make a point of forcing watermelons to grow very early, but the result of my labor was insipid fruit. Citrus growers have found that while an orange will grow in a certain area it will not develop the same sweetness and flavor as one grown where the total growing temperature units are a few hundred degrees higher. Lastly, air temperature governs soil temperature, and if roots are to grow, there must be adequate heat both above and below the ground.

The warm weather crops are particularly susceptible to lack of soil heat. Time and again I've attempted to plant squash or corn in cold, clammy ground only to have the seeds rot before they germinate. No matter what the air temperature, the seeds of corn and tomato have a difficult time germinating before the soil reaches 50°. Melons, squashes, pumpkins, peppers, okra, eggplant, beans, and cucumbers all germinate around 60°. We can beat the cold ground of spring by germinating seed indoors and transplanting, but some crops, like corn, resist transplanting. To start them indoors would be costly in materials, time consuming, and not necessarily successful. Those directions on the seed packets that say, "Plant when all danger of frost is past, and the ground is warmed up," mean just that. (To tell when the ground is warm without a thermometer, every week beginning in February or March thrust your hand into the soil and take note of the sensation of cold. When the soil warms up you'll know the difference. It will "feel" right, just like bath water "feels" right for a bath. If this sounds unclear now don't worry, it will be clear when you do it.)

There are many ways to hasten the warming-up process or compensate for the cold. One is to draw back any mulch. This gives the sun direct contact with the soil. Another way is to plow or harrow the soil. This stirring causes the ground to warm more quickly. Third, for early plantings pick slope exposures in this order— south, southeast, southwest, east, west. Fourth, pick a light, sandy soil in preference to a heavy clay. By light I mean in texture, not in color, though the two often go together.

You can also cover seed and young plants with hotcaps, gallon bottles with the bottoms cut out, or cloches especially made for the purpose. I've used this cover-up method both to give starting plants a warm environment and to protect them from cutworms. Take care not to let the leaves touch the sides of the glass as they can burn, or worse, contract fungus or mildew diseases in the humid, quiet air in the cloche. Also on hot days it can get very hot inside the glass and wilt tender plants. A last way to raise temperatures outdoors is black plastic mulch. I've never used it but the field station reports I've read indicate that unrolling plastic over the earth and making slits for the crop to grow through the plastic eliminates weeds, conserves moisture, and warms up the ground considerably. It can be rolled up and reused in subsequent seasons.

In this chapter I'll discuss in further detail the effects of heat on specific crops and how I've dealt with this and other factors to produce optimum vegetables. I've arranged the sections beginning with those warm weather crops that stand the most cold. The order is not absolute, merely an indication of hardiness. I have deliberately left out some crops—okra and sweet potatoes being two notable examples—because my experience with them is limited to the fact that I've tried to grow them and have found my climate unsuitable.

Corn: The Gambler's Life

What would summer be without sweet corn? As far as I'm concerned this native American crop is one of the most important vegetables in this country and deserves a space in any garden, no matter how small. The nice thing about corn is you can't waste it. If you eat it sweet you have a fresh vegetable. If it goes beyond the sugar stage you can let it dry, grind it up, and you have cornmeal. Cattle

177

will eat the green stalks, you can compost the remains and return it to the field, or—using power equipment—you can turn it under as sheet compost after grinding.

I learned to grow and use corn from a lot of farmers who plowed the earth ahead of me and I find myself learning new ways every season—most of them concerned with two aspects of the art of gardening: getting a crop in the earliest possible time, and getting the highest return from a given plot of ground for a given crop.

Now it didn't take me long to figure out that anybody could grow corn. I remember as a kid I had a limited garden space so I decided to plant corn along a creek bank near our house. All I did was sow the corn in bare ground and let it go. Come harvest time there were a few small plants that had survived the vicissitudes of poor soil, inadequate irrigation, weeds, and general neglect. My lesson was that anyone can grow corn, but not everyone is going to get a decent crop. There's more to corn than the instructions on the seed packet if you're interested in the kind of production I like.

I always waited for the ground to get reasonably warm before planting, knowing that below 50° soil temperature corn will either rot or refuse to germinate until it gets warmer. Then I met a lady who truck farms some fairly decent bench land along the Eel River about thirty miles upstream of our place in Loleta. Her name's Mary Hansen and she knows her corn. I hired out to her hoeing weeds in six-inch-high corn one spring day and we got to talking about why her corn was already well up while ours wasn't even out of the ground yet. I mentioned that one of her neighbors across the river had told me that in the ten years he'd been living in the little community of Pepperwood just across the river none of the truck farmers would tell him the varieties of corn they used. (Pepperwood and Shively are the major fresh-vegetable-growing areas on the Humboldt coast and the local growers are so competitive they don't tell each other what they're growing so they can corner the high-return early market for themselves.)

Mrs. Hansen said growing for the early market depends on two factors: one is gambling on the weather; the other is having an early seed suited to the climate.

The first is an educated guess every year. Shively has a very temperate climate. Like Loleta it doesn't get too hot or too cold, but it does experience some hard, cold, driving rainstorms that can turn a newly planted field into a mud flow in a few hours. There's also the chance of the usual spring rains not coming at all, but rather a hot, drying wind blowing steadily up the river valley.

What usually happens, though, is a break in the rains sometime in March, and for the farmer with friable soil it's possible after a few days of warm weather to plow, disc, and harrow a small field, and put in a crop. Naturally it's a gamble, especially if you plant shallow, because a storm could come up and wash your seedbed down the river, the weather could turn sullen and stay that way until your seed rotted in the ground, or it could turn dry and your stand could get half-started and wilt if you couldn't get water to it.

The second factor, good, early seed, can be established through years of experimentation. Once you find a good variety, stick with it, but keep up small experimental plots every year in the hope of finding something better. Mrs. Hansen had two early corns. One is a type I was already using, but she was particular about where she got hers—it was from Joseph Harris Seed Co. because that company specializes in strains suited to harsh New England and Canadian conditions. She figured such seed would be an advantage. Personally, I have two favorite varieties: Early Sunglow, which has proven itself time and again in various conditions, and Royal Crest, which comes in back to back with Sunglow and allows me a quick succession harvest from one planting. There may be others you'll find more adaptable to your climate.

I must admit that I'm drawn to planting early corn. If all goes well I have corn on the table and in the market before everyone else and I have nothing to lose except a few bucks worth of seed and a little time.

As soon as weather permits after the first of March I turn over the ground and prepare a seedbed. I consider it essential to stir up the ground for an early spring crop because there's no corn seed I know that will germinate in cold, clammy ground. Permanent mulches are strictly out for early corn. My soil has a clay rather than sand base, so I choose a section that has loads of organic matter on the basis that it's light and will warm quickly, giving me the advantage of a sandy loam.

Corn is a very heavy nitrogen feeder and also needs significant amounts of phosphorus for optimum ear growth. Compost and manure are the logical ways to provide both these nutrients and I add them just before I plow or spade the ground. It's almost impossible to give corn too much fertilizer. Seven hundred fifty to 1,000 pounds per 1,000 square feet is reasonable for top production, especially with the later, larger-growing varieties. I also add enough dolomite to keep the pH between 6 and 6.5. Once or twice in my life I've been forced by extraordinary circumstances to use chemical nitrogen, but I'm convinced that besides the sin of not adding humus to the soil, chemicals promote lush, quick growth at the expense of the overall health of the plant. Agroscientists have demonstrated that noxious insects actually have some sense about which are the lush, nutritionally overbalanced plants, and attack them. So if you use chemicals you're just asking for trouble.

Soaking the corn overnight is a necessity, and I've even taken it a step further by sprouting seed. This latter practice requires care, and I'm lucky to have a wife who's a good sprouter and who diligently rinses the seed four times a day. When the corn shows the first signs of sprouting, plant. At times I've been a little slow and have found that once corn starts sending out a shoot it doesn't like to be disturbed. In Washington a friend gave me some seeds with sprouts an inch long. Despite my care and watering most of the crop failed to break the surface. I've determined therefore to watch for the first signs of germination and plant. Even then it may be a long time before the seedlings show.

Depth is a difficult question. If I plant at the usual one and one-half inches it's possible that cold, damp weather will cause the seed to rot. If I plant at one-half inch there's the chance of a heavy rain washing the seed away. So I compromise at one inch. A storm heavy enough to float a seed from a one-inch depth will most likely float a seed from one and one-half inches too in these parts. Make no mistake about it if you opt for a shallow depth at any time of the year: seeds will work themselves to the top if there's a lot of water. Then you'll be feeding the crows.

The next question is "hills or rows?" I solve that by deciding on the use I intend to put the patch to. My early corn is often support for late peas or early beans and I find row planting works fine. I plant in blocks to insure good pollination which in turn means well-filled ears.

My mid-season and late corn fulfill two purposes. In one instance the stalks become supports for beans so I plant them in rows. In the other, the corn plot is also the squash and pumpkin patch. Sometimes, if I'm using a wide-spaced corn like late popcorn, I plant in rows and let the pumpkins run between. Otherwise I plant to have three plants to a hill (that means sow five seeds and thin if necessary), with the hills spaced three feet in every direction, and I let the pumpkins ramble through. I'm happy with two crops from one area, the corn is happy with a living mulch, and the pumpkins are happy with a light shade.

There's one other scheme that's caught my fancy lately. Somebody gave me a packet of Northrup's Golden Hybrid NK199, and the directions said to sow two seeds within six inches and then skip twenty inches and repeat the process, and so on down each three-foot-wide row. After testing I modified that to three seeds within six inches and thinning when necessary. When the corn first comes up it looks like a whole lot of wasted space. In fact it's almost embarrassing to look at because it appears the planting was so slipshod that most of the crop didn't come up. This is excellent space for young squashes and pumpkins to get started in. The interesting part about NK199 is that it thinks nothing of growing eight or nine feet tall, and what looks like wasted space in May is actually just right come tassling time.

Getting back to my March corn (April where the ground freezes in winter as my Washington garden did), I plant soaked seed every three inches and thin to every twelve inches in rows two and one-half feet apart. I've planted as close as eighteen inches but I don't see any gain in that, especially since by widening up a little I can get peas or beans in and still use much less room than either would individually take. There are some folks who space at six inches in the rows with early types. This is good if you're working in raised beds or wherever else you have fine control over the variables. For field-sown corn: two feet if you're not going to intercrop, and two and one-half feet if you are, thinned to stand nine to twelve inches in the row.

Do your first thinning and weeding at the same time, when the corn's just about six inches high. By the time the corn is twelve inches the weather will have warmed up considerably and you'll be ready to put on a side-dressing of rotted manure if you have it, or fish emulsion if you don't.

I cultivate in a very particular way. I don't get too close to the root system because it tends to spread laterally just below the surface. What I do is draw dirt from the center of the rows up and around the plants, covering the base. This gives additional support for the plant and a place for the secondary root system to take root. I don't bother removing sucker growth. It takes too much time and I've never noticed any difference in yield. After this, if the soil is really warm I add a very light mulch—just enough to break up the drying effect of the wind and sun on the soil.

I water whenever the top inch of soil appears dry, and prefer a high overhead system so the water drops down easily like rain, and doesn't run smack into the corn when it's seven feet tall. Adjustable Rainbird sprinklers on posts suit my needs well. A few of them with a length of flexible hose will cover the stand in a couple days. Corn, contrary to popular opinion, is not a shallow-rooted crop, so it pays to be sure that the soil is wet to a depth of eight inches with each irrigation.

Some of my neighbors prefer furrow irrigation, which is also an excellent method, but without mechanical equipment I find that too much labor, even though they claim to get better root aeration. On flat ground I've seen people make dikes all around the stand and flood it like a rice paddy. This idea requires very little water manipulation, but if there's squash growing among the corn there's a real possibility of rot.

There's some controversy about watering during tassling time. My personal opinion, and this is where gardening gets to be a very subjective art, is that if the corn needs water as it tassels, give it a good soaking, but don't water at all when the silk is coming out. Right or wrong, I believe that dry pollen falling from the tassels to dry silk provides better pollination and therefore better-filled ears. Once the silks start turning brown on the tips I water again as needed, with that one inch of dry topsoil my indicator.

It's such a joy to see mature, deep green sweet corn with two or more well-formed ears nearly bursting off of each stalk. I select a test ear from a seemingly ripe stand, pull the husk back slightly, and with my thumbnail press into a kernel. The day my nail splits the skin and a creamy juice squirts out it's picking time and my extra early corn is in. The best harvesting instruction I've encountered is this: "Don't pick until the water is boiling." Corn, except for a few new hybrids, passes from the sweet "milk" stage to a starchy "dough" stage often within a day of picking, with a marked loss of flavor and tenderness. When it's ready, it's ready for only a few days in the field, and you have to eat, sell, freeze, or can it on the spot. Otherwise let it turn to dry corn for parching or meal.

As for the later corns, I plant them in just about the same way beginning when the weather is warm in May. Since I have a hard time making successive plantings I've worked out a system whereby I sow nearly all my corn at one time, each having a different maturity date. For example, I resow blocks of Early Sunglow and Royal Crest, then add Butterfingers, Sunburst, Golden Cross Bantam, Black Aztec, and Country Gentleman, giving me a continuous harvest from between 65 and 105 days under optimum conditions. You can see a May planting sets me up into September. The only other work I have to do is replant two more varieties like Sunglow and Bantam in July and my harvest will extend up to November when the rains effectively stop growth anyway. This staggered harvest also saves me (actually my wife) the pressure of having to can or freeze all the corn at once.

At the end of the season I prefer to compost the stalks, but it's fine to shred and plow them under. The main point is not to give pests a breeding place. A leguminous cover crop, green-manured in the spring, helps to renew the nutrients that were removed, though I add some rock phosphate broadcast. To further insure fertility and to give the land a rest from corn I plant a crop like carrots the following year, then beans or peas, and only then do I return to corn. As the days come when manures and compost ingredients get harder to find I think legumes and green manures will provide much of the answer to maintaining corn production.

All the corn commonly grown can be broken down

into five basic categories—field, sweet, pop, parching, and ornamental. The first type is for animal feed and forage; the others we grow in our gardens according to the purposes their names imply. Of the sweet corns the early sorts don't generally grow more than four feet high and have small ears. For my main crop my three choices are Golden Bantam Cross, Black Aztec, and Country Gentleman. They are good fresh, frozen, canned, or dried, and produce considerably more than earlier corns per plant, having deeper kernels and longer ears with more rows. My choice for cornmeal and for the best all-around eating corn is Black Aztec. It's sweet, and beautiful, and the kernels mature to a sort of bluish charcoal that lend themselves to decorative uses. Country Gentleman is sweet too—an old-fashioned "shoepeg" corn that's been around as long as anyone living today. Some folks object that its white kernels lack the vitamin content of the yellow corns, but I say if you're growing an organic garden and eating plenty of produce you're getting more than enough vitamins and minerals anyway. Cream-style Country Gentleman makes my mouth water, whether fresh or fresh-from-the jar in mid-winter.

Of the popcorns I choose South American hybrid, also known as Dynamite. It's a long-season crop (105 days or more), but I get upwards of three ears off each stalk when all goes right and the kernels pop large. Sometimes I plant the popular Japanese Hull-less, which matures nearly three months earlier, just to have some popcorn to tide me over until the main crop, but it doesn't have near the production of the South American types.

One thing to remember about all popcorn is that it takes anywhere from two to six months for the moisture content to adjust itself after the initial field drying before it will pop. I don't have any explanation for this phenomenon. So don't be discouraged if your popcorn hardly pops the first few months. Give it time and it will.

Of the decorative corns there're two I'd like to mention in particular, Calico and Strawberry. By the time you get tired of looking at them hanging on the wall or in a centerpiece they'll be ready for popping. That's a double-edged selling point, too.

I make a particular point to test new corns every season, and most recently had five blocks growing of types I'd never personally seen growing before. I also try different fertilizer and cultural practices as I think them up or hear of them. This is the only way I know to improve the quality of my garden and gardening. Corn is a particularly exciting crop to experiment with because as a native plant it has thousands of possibilities for Western Hemisphere farming locked into its genetic structure. Who knows—one of us might just come across the all-time miracle corn for all seasons everywhere. Or is that simply the musing of a summertime roast-corn-on-the-cob lover?

New Zealand Spinach

On his circumnavigation of the world, Captain James Cook put into Queen Charlotte Sound on New Zealand's South Island, and a group of men went ashore. Among them was the naturalist Sir Joseph Banks. Whether because one of the native Maoris recommended it, or because he was an adventurous wild-food gatherer at heart, Sir Joseph tasted one of the plants growing there, liked it, found that it helped prevent scurvy, and took it back to England. From there its use spread throughout the western world as a warm weather substitute for spinach: hence its name, New Zealand spinach. It's native to many islands of the Eastern Pacific where, along with several of its relatives like the sea fig and ice plant, it's either cultivated or picked from the wild for its edible tender stalks and leaves.

I got involved with it one year when I took part in a community garden. Jay Sooter suggested growing it as a cash crop. What impressed me was not its saleability, but how easily it transplanted and how fast it grew. When I moved about seventy-five miles up the coast to a garden just above the ocean on the south edge of Humboldt Bay I found that New Zealand spinach thrived as well in the fog as it did in the sun.

One autumn I turned over a section of garden where New Zealand spinach had been planted and sowed rye. That was the last I thought about it until the next March when Tom Becotte called me out of the house to witness an unusual discovery. He had been rototilling the rye under in preparation for spring planting when he came across several New Zealand spinach plants. The rye had overgrown them and protected them from the winter frosts. Though their leaves were a little yellowed and ragged, they still made fine greens, and certainly convinced me of their hardiness. In fact, New Zealand spinach should find a place in every garden even if the most you can give it is a five-gallon container filled with compost hanging along a south wall. Because of its prostrate creeping habit it can be trained to go up and around most anything.

Culture is very simple. When the ground is warm soak the tough-coated seeds in warm water overnight, and sow one every three inches. Thin to stand twelve inches to two feet in rows four feet wide. You can plant lettuce, turnips, or some other quick crop to within fifteen inches of the spinach as they will be long gone before the latter needs the space. I find it advisable to work a spadeful of compost into every square foot of planting row, along with a dusting of lime. When the stems start to radiate I mulch with an airy mulch like hay, and side-dress with a half-cup of bloodmeal around each plant. I water when the soil under the mulch dries out a half-inch.

Where water is in short supply this is one crop that will stand a long time between waterings. I pick the tender growing tips when the plants have spread about eighteen inches. The more you pick them the more the stems will branch and the more tender tips there will be to eat. Given time and not-too-drastic harvesting, the plants can spread out ten feet. The older leaves and stems get quite tough and should be left on the plant unless they're growing out of bounds. The plants will continue to grow and yield right up to the first killing frost with very little care. If there are any bugs or diseases that attack them I don't know about them.

As the plants grow they set a profusion of tiny yellow green flowers which you hardly notice unless you're looking. You also don't notice the huge amount of seeds one of these plants produces in a season immediately, but the next spring you will. Volunteers will spring up all over the last year's patch. It's a very easy matter to dig them up and transplant them wherever you want. They hardly suffer a setback. I've discovered it's easier if you transplant after the seedlings are more than a couple of inches tall, pinching the whole plant back to the side shoot closest to the roots, which will become the new main shoot as the plant becomes established. By this method I've moved plants that were spreading out two feet. You have to take care to get as much of the extensive root system as possible. It doesn't hurt to bury part of the stem of older plants.

If you want a real head start on the season you can start your plants anytime after January in deep flats. When you cut them back to plant you have your first harvest from the thinnings. I wouldn't hesitate to transplant hardened-off New Zealand spinach into field rows a week after the last average frost date. They won't show much growth until the weather warms up, but the root systems will be established and ready to produce when seed that is field-planted hasn't yet broken the surface.

Worth A Hill of Beans

Whoever originated the expression that something isn't "worth a hill of beans," must not have been a farmer because a farmer knows that beans contribute greatly to the world's health and economy. In Latin America the staples are corn and beans, two vegetables whose amino acids complement each other to produce more usable protein than either alone. In the Orient the staples are rice and beans. Beans are a direct source of protein in a world where well over a billion people are malnourished by American standards and 120 million die of starvation every year.

We in the United States don't often think of ourselves as bean consumers, but when you think about how many products come from just one species like the soybean you begin to see we're more dependent on beans than we thought. From the soybean we get oil for cooking and margarine, vegetable protein products used as meat extenders or meat substitutes, lecithin for cooking and as a dietary supplement, soy sauces and tofu, soy nut snacks, and meat from cattle that were fed partially on soybeans and its derivatives.

Some kinds of beans—the soy for example—have been cultivated in Asia for thousands of years and only recently have been introduced to the Americas. However, most of the major cultivated beans in the world today were unknown outside of the Americas before Columbus arrived. These include snap and field beans, limas, and scarlet runners, and will be the major topic of this discussion.

In one form or another these beans are adaptable to every climate where there's three months of frost-free weather with a minimum temperature average of around

55°. Because they add nitrogen to the soil through the efforts of bacteria in their root nodules they improve the quality of the land. They also add significant amounts of humus.

I grow beans everywhere. I plant bush beans and halfrunners in their own rows, and pole beans and pinto around corn, sunflowers, or on trellises and poles. If I had a small garden I would choose pole beans and locate them along the north side where they wouldn't shade the other crops. They are more economical space users than bush beans because they grow vertically, and because they begin bearing in about two-and-a-half months and continue until frost nips them. The bush bean produces for only a month, but its advantage is that some varieties mature a full two weeks ahead of the earliest pole beans. You can pick the bushes, and when the yields begin to drop off, turn them under, thus enriching the soil, and plant another vegetable. Another advantage with bush beans is that you don't have to give them support. Sometimes I have so much other work to do that if I had to get all my beans up on poles or trellises, I wouldn't be able to plant as many.

To plant bush or halfrunner beans I select a fairly fertile soil. The only fertilizer I add is about three pounds of rock phosphate per 100 feet of row. Beans will take nitrogen from the soil at first, but if it's in good condition, as when a thick mulch has been turned under along with the residue of the previous crop, the plants will thrive on what the soil bacteria have released, and later they will produce their own nitrogen. I assume that I have enough potash from natural sources like seaweed mulches. Elsewhere you might want to add a pound of wood ashes or bone meal to the phosphorus application. Lime is rarely necessary. Beans thrive in a soil with a pH as low as 5.5. I sow bush beans an inch apart in rows eighteen inches apart. I always water down the soil the day before and soak the seed overnight.

Inoculation is a must if the plot hasn't already been

grown to inoculated beans.* It's very important to keep the seedbed soil loose. In Bridgeport, my helper Jim Boutcher and I couldn't figure out what was taking our beans so long to surface. Finally Jim started digging down the rows with a trowel to see if the seed had rotted. It turned out the surface soil had crusted and the big bean cotyledon leaves were having a difficult time breaking through. Working over the surface with a garden rake helped some in that situation, but had we forseen the problem we would have made a fifty-fifty mixture of sand and dirt to sift over the seeds at planting time.

Don't plant before the ground is warm; the seed will rot. When the plants are up and have put out their first true leaves I cultivate shallowly, drawing a little dirt around the stems. It's also time to apply a very light moisture-conserving mulch. After the plants are about four inches high and I don't have to worry about cutworms anymore I thin to four inches in the rows. When the plants are half grown I cultivate for the last time, drawing still more soil around them, and I apply a mulch to the depth of three or four inches.

Harvest time is when the beans in the pods barely show their outline. They soon get tough. If you want to keep them producing for a few weeks it's important to pick all the beans that are ready. I go through the rows about every three days. Production wanes after about a week, but a secondary crop comes through. As soon as it looks like the crop is definitely diminishing, or even before that point if I'm pressed to get another vegetable in, I turn under the crop. In a couple weeks I'm ready to sow a fall crop.

Among the varieties I like Topcrop, Commodore, and Tenderbest for green snap beans. Pencil Pod Black Wax is my choice among the yellow snap beans. With over 2,000 varieties of beans in the world, and new ones

---

*Inoculation, as explained earlier, is simply coating the seeds with a commercially prepared nitrogen-fixing bacteria strain.

being developed every year, there's considerable room for experimentation until you find the beans that grow best in your garden. I figure on planting 100 feet of row with a half-pound of seed. This should yield 75 to 100 pounds of produce. It takes about 2 pounds of beans to make a quart of canned or frozen beans.

Culture of the halfrunners is the same as for bush beans except that they require more space between rows. I've planted them as an alternative to having to erect poles or wires for pole beans. Black-eyed peas, though from a different genus than the snap beans, require the same culture as the halfrunners, and also a bit more heat. I mention them here because as fresh "shell beans" they're hard to beat, especially when cooked with butter, diced bacon, and sautéed onion.

While there are several different species of pole beans I'm only going to discuss the snap beans and the runners. They have identical habits, but the scarlet runner has the advantage of being more resistant to cold weather and adverse conditions. The European explorers who first reached the north Atlantic seaboard found the Indians there cultivating runner beans but none of the others because the climate was too harsh. The scarlet runner is very prolific and very dependable in the cool end of the bean range. It has one normally cultivated cousin, the White Dutch Runner. I grow runners for dried use only, but I grow snap beans for both fresh and dried use. The common snap bean is good as a snap bean, as a fresh-shelled bean (but not as good as the black-eyed pea), and as a baking or soup bean. In fact the kidneys, navys, pinto, and many other dried beans are snap beans that have matured and dried. Of the soup types I grow only Pintos. They are reliable, heavy yielders, and have the best taste of any dried bean I've ever grown. Among the snap beans I plant Kentucky Wonder. It's a wonderful strain for fresh or dried use.

With all of them the first consideration is support. All beans, bush or pole, are sensitive to bacterial blight, to anthracnose fungus, and to downy mildew. One of the greatest causes of the spread of these diseases is gardeners cultivating or harvesting when the plants are wet. The diseases spread from plant to plant on wet clothes or implements. Therefore no work should be done on beans when the plants are wet from rain, irrigation, or dew. Pole beans should be securely raised up off the ground because sprawling, jumbled vines are surely going to be the ones that permit disease to enter the garden. In harvesting other peoples' beans for cannery use I've come across case after case of mildew infestations that I'm certain could have been avoided by the use of poles. The commercial growers often try to get past the disease problem with lots of pesticides.

My preference for poles is a natural one—cornstalks. This is a time-honored Central and South American Indian way of growing beans from the very people who have been doing it longer than anyone. As I never get tired of repeating, beans and corn go together. The catch is that in the tropics beans can follow corn, thereby returning to the soil some of the nitrogen the corn removed. In our short growing seasons we have to grow corn and beans concurrently.

Here there are two choices. One is to grow an extra early corn as early as possible, and when it's about two feet high sow five beans around the base of each corn, thinning to the best three. By the time the corn is harvested, the beans will be growing, albeit slowly because of the shade. At that point cut away some of the corn foliage and you now have bean poles. The other method is to sow the beans when the corn is six inches high. If you sow earlier the beans will outstrip the corn and cause a great confusion. I find this method good for main-season corn and beans I intend to dry on the vines. I've also tried beans and sunflowers and it works, but I have to sacrifice sunflower productivity by spacing them wider apart and by stripping the leaves from the lower stems to make room for the beans to climb. Sunflowers also make a very dense shade under their leaf canopy in normal or close spacing.

Of the artificial supports, I've tried three and they all have their merits. One is to make tripods about six feet tall at the apex with about four feet between the legs. Plant five seeds and thin to the best three around each pole. This is a very easy arrangement to pick, and you can grow rows of roots, greens, or cucumbers (an especially good choice) beneath. Second is the old-fashioned pole. I plant this way when space is at a premium. I put the poles three feet apart and eighteen inches in the rows, with three or four plants to each pole. Last is what I consider the ideal method, and that's to grow all the beans three inches apart on trellises. This results in maximum use of space, but it also takes the most material. My trellises have been wood frames six feet high with sisal tied tautly top and bottom every three inches. To further strengthen the network I run more sisal horizontally every twelve inches. The trouble is that sisal lasts one season and has a tendency to flex in the wind. Wire instead of sisal would be better and more permanent, the best being something like chicken wire six feet tall.

I recommend successive plantings for fresh eating and one big planting for processing. A total of a 100 feet of row should be enough for both uses for the average family. If you're growing dry beans let them remain on the vine until the pods are just about dry, then pick and further dry and thresh or shell. In my climate I allow the beans to dry as far as they can on the vines because there's no danger of the pods splitting. Elsewhere you might want to finish drying on a threshing floor.

Whether you grow for fresh or dried use it's important that you realize that you're not adding a great amount of nitrogen to the soil. Nitrogen-fixing bacteria will add significant amounts of this element to the soil, but when you harvest the beans you take off twice as much nitrogen in the form of pods and beans as you leave behind in leaves and stems. This could mean ninety-five pounds or more to the acre, depending on conditions. The bacteria might not fix much more than that. Thus there would be a net gain in humus but no significant gain in available nitrogen for the next crop, and an actual loss of all the other nutrients. There is a world of difference between an unharvested crop of beans grown as a green manure, and a crop that is harvested and turned under.

Still, the bean is more a soil-enriching than a soil-depleting crop. It has the advantage of not requiring very much available nitrogen for its initial growth, the bacteria add significant amounts, and overall your garden does have more total nitrogen in the sense that if another crop were growing in that spot you would definitely have to fertilize before planting. The bean manufactures its own supply. The point is that the crop that follows beans should receive a normal application of fertilizer for it to give optimum results. Viewed this way, the bean forms a strong link in a homestead cycle of use, growth, and reuse, and is a significant helper in building the organic quality of our lives.

Tomatoes:
The Gardener's Tour de Force

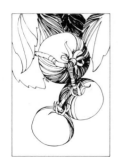

The tomato is king of the garden. People who wouldn't raise a radish nevertheless pick up a flat of tomatoes at the local market every spring and grow a crop for home eating. Among gardeners there are so many techniques and so many theories about this crop from sowing to storage that a person could spend an entire season just reading the literature and never plant a seed.

I know I get the tomato urge every year and in every climate where I've lived—even the nigh impossible damp one along the ocean. One year I recall being so excited about an early warm spell in January that I planted seed in the open. None came up except one Pearson's Improved that made its appearance in May and eventually out-produced all the transplants I painstakingly started indoors.

With that Pearson's in mind I want to quote from the book, *Making Horticulture Pay*, by M. G. Kains. Back in 1909 he said, "To grow tomatoes requires no special skill. In fact, there is no plant in field or garden except the weed that will submit to gross neglect as will the tomato and if we were content to grow a supply for home or market during the months of August and September no especial instruction or costly manipulation would be required." While I'm not prepared to state that the tomato is the most tolerant of adverse conditions, I agree in principle with Kains. The point is that we are not inclined to grow this plant in its natural climate and season. We want fruit all year around, and that takes knowledge. I intend to discuss only my ways of producing this plant as I believe the principles behind them are the same as those behind the scores of other workable methods.

The tomato is a tropical American plant, and as such it grows as a perennial. This need for heat carries into modern culture. With the possible exception of the variety Cold Set, tomatoes will not tolerate frost. When the temperature drops to 32° they turn black and die. Where nighttime temperatures consistently dip below 60° the blossoms will open, but drop off before fruit sets.

Length of season plays an important part in tomato production. The average variety takes about fourteen weeks to grow outdoors from seed to first ripe fruit under warm conditions. In the fog belt I've waited more than three months for fruit from transplants to ripen. Obviously where the growing season is short you have to start plants indoors and transplant after the danger of frost is past. The tomato doesn't germinate until the ground temperature is about 50°. Even a tomato that's transplanted will languish, or worse, be subject to insect and disease losses, if the ground is cold, even though frost danger is over. What this plant wants is an optimum average temperature between 70° and 75°. Curiously enough, it suffers from too much heat as well as from too little. If the daytime temperature soars into the 90s for several days the blossoms will start dropping. And when the daily mean temperature is above 70° the fruit that ripens during that time will be off-color, mushy, and not at all pleasing to the taste. It's impossible to cover every temperature situation, especially when you have a large garden and the plants are full grown. Commercially available "blossom-set" hormone mixes probably help control fruit losses to some extent, but I take into account my environment and the needs of the plant, and proceed as if nothing unusual will happen.

I grow two types of tomatoes, early and late. The early ones are often of the determinate type—that is, they grow, blossom, and set fruit. At that point most foliage growth stops and the plant directs its energy into producing a ripe crop. Main-season crops are mostly of the indeterminate type. They continue to grow, blossom, and to mature fruit all at once. They bear continually until frost kills them.

To grow an early crop I need three things: an early variety, an early start, and an early ground. In the first case, as with corn, I've not found the perfect variety. Fireball at sixty days to maturity after being set out and Earliana at sixty-five days are the two I've had the most success with. A cherry tomato called Subarctic matures twenty days earlier than these two, but it's not a big, slicing variety. The early ground is the sunniest sheltered place in the garden—the south side of a fence is a good choice. Unfortunately I have just so much such space, and a lot of crops that benefit by being there. I find it important to get early plants up in the air. Those that sprawl on the ground mature two weeks later than staked plants.

I start early varieties about the middle of February. Tomatoes are very responsive to light and heat so I pay close attention to temperatures. The best daytime temperature is about 65° to 70° with a night temperature between 60° to 65°. Growth is very regular but not rapid as it would be with a higher temperature. I make sure to put them where they will get a minimum six hours of sunlight a day. I've used hot frames and south windows to germinate seed and grow young plants. The window-sill method works fine if you turn the flat a quarter turn each day so they won't grow up leaning in one direction with most of their leaf growth to one side. A grow-lamp is a good investment for folks with limited natural light sources.

The other things I do to insure an early start for tomatoes are the same things I do for main season varieties. Thus, I'll treat them together with the understanding that I sow the earlies in flats about two weeks before the lates, and transplant them to the field two weeks earlier. My choices for main-season tomatoes are purely West Coast local. I like Ace. My second choice (first if I lived in a hot climate) is Pearson's Improved. It's prolific and tasty. From time to time I also grow San Marzano, a first-class sauce and puree maker. Every area of the country will have varieties suited to the local climate, so it's best to check with local agricultural extension services, and with successful gardeners in your areas, as well as to experiment.

The value of growing your own seed, by the way, is that you can select the varieties you want to grow and do it without chemicals. An ounce of seed that costs about two dollars will yield 4,000 plants. This gives you an idea of how ridiculously cheap it is in comparison to started plants that cost up to four dollars a dozen through seed catalogs. Even if you buy seed in small packets you should be able to get nearly 200 plants from each, and you don't have to use it all at once. Seed stored in a cool dry place should give good germination and vigorous plants for four years. I've used egg cartons to start small amounts of seed, placing three seeds in each compartment, and then separating the excess into other egg cartons. Other folks use milk cartons cut lengthwise for starter flats, and cartons cut in half for individual plants. In any case sow seed indoors about four to six weeks before the last expected frost date, to be set out two weeks after that date as the ground is warming up.

When the seedlings are about two and a half inches high, transplant them to stand at least two by two inches in the flats. When they're four to five inches high you can transplant them to three-inch clay or peat pots or tin cans. The resulting plants will be very stocky. They should be put in a cool place for a few days with a maximum temperature of 60°, and then a few more days with a 55° temperature. This won't stop growth but it will slow it down and make your plants able to withstand the outdoor environment. Whenever the weather is good set them outdoors. Protect them on cold nights and on gusty, rainy, or chilly days. Most of the time I omit the transplanting to three-inch pots, but that's because I start my plants at a time of year when growth is very slow because of the low light intensity. If I started them a month later as most people do, I would probably opt for the double transplants before setting them out.

If you're only planting a couple dozen, and that should be enough for fresh use for the average family (fifty plants if you plant to can), I suggest using peat pots. The plants get a much quicker start in the field when their roots aren't disturbed. If you're planting up in the hundreds you might want to consider the cost, but again a quicker maturing plant can mean dollars of income that more than offsets the cost of pots. Early tomatoes almost always command a premium price in the local market. Watering in the flats should be light but adequate, or the

199

plants will get leggy. If the base of the stem is showing a little purple color you're doing the job right. Ideally every transplant should be strong and stocky. To achieve this, keep the plant close to the glass, and don't give it too much water, nutrients, or heat. If you use flats all the way through, make sure that you block off the plants about a week to five days before you transplant to the field. This is simply the process of cutting through the soil between the plants as I outlined for lettuce. (see page 123)

The outdoor bed should be in as sunny a spot as possible. I dig a hole twelve inches wide, and at least as deep, and fill it with water that I then allow to completely percolate down. After that, I fill the hole halfway with compost and one-third cup of rock phosphate, and mix in enough dirt to bring it to the soil surface level. Finally, I water again. I don't add limestone because the tomato does quite well in any soil between pH 5.5 and 6.8. I've mentioned elsewhere that an excess of nitrogen will cause the tomato to put its energy into lush growth instead of fruit production. If you feel you have to add anything extra, make it natural phosphate and potash.

I used to be very conservative about transplanting, but now, thanks to Max Sikstrom, who's one of the most agriculturally radical men I've ever met, I'm a bit daring too.

He was looking around the garden I had up in Bridgeport one day as I was setting out tomatoes. Quite abruptly he turned and asked, "Do you want to grow the best tomatoes you ever grew?"

"Sure," I answered.

His steel blue eyes fixed on mine. He knows I'm very tenderhearted toward vegetables. "You have to prune them down to nothing."

I've seen Max do some innovative things, like lay out his pear orchard like a hedgerow, fight fire blight with fire, and put in drip-irrigated orchards on land other growers thought was too steep for fruit, so though I was hesitant, I paid attention. "How?"

"Do you mind?" He took a vigorous Ace and deftly pinched off all but the two large leaves at the tip and whatever leaflets were left by the terminal bud. He buried the result to within two inches of the top. "This is how I grew tomatoes commercially. The stem underground will turn into roots. The vines will be bushy and sturdy. Do you have the nerve to do it?"

"I've got half the nerve," I replied. There didn't seem to be much left of my once-leafy Ace. Gamely I followed his instructions with over two hundred plants, about half my patch that year. They were stockier, less sprawly, and bore as much fruit as my usual transplants. Until I experiment more I can't say I've settled on Max's way totally, but I think there is wisdom in heavy transplant pruning. After that initial pruning I let all the plants go their own way.

Another gardener I know grows his tomatoes on the same ground every year. He says they like it that way. I take a slightly different view: A heavy continual cropping creates an imbalance of soil nutrients and also leads to the possibility of a buildup of disease organisms.

"In an organic garden?" he parried. "With seaweed mulches and fish emulsion fertilizers? Are you kidding? Tomatoes grow better in the same ground and that's a fact you can demonstrate to yourself by doing it. Organic methods will keep them healthy."

"It's hard to believe," I said.

"Do it this way, then. Compost your vines, and put the stuff on next year's tomatoes. Half a loaf is better than none."

So that's what I now do.

Early varieties like Fireball are very compact in their habits and easily fit into three- by four-foot rows. The late varieties need at least four by four feet if they're allowed to sprawl. There's plenty of room for other crops at first, and in fact I start greens about a month before I transplant the tomatoes. They're gone before the latter need the space. I deeply mulch with a light material like hay or straw as this solves many of the problems associated with fruit rot.

A variation on this method, and one that I think preferable, is to make hogwire circles about three feet in diameter with the plant in the middle. The plant will grow bushy and erect. As with all sprawl methods the hard part is finding the fruit as it ripens. It takes a sharp eye and a lot of leafing through the foliage. The advantage of these nonpruning sprawl techniques are many. First of all there's no labor involved in staking, trellising, or pruning. (The latter, by the way, is not a one-time process but must be continued throughout the season with all nondeterminate strains or they will get sprawly even if staked.) Blossom-end rot is less with sprawl tomatoes, production is greater per plant, and the fruit suffers less from sunscald and splitting because of the amount of foliage covering the plant.

Where space is at a premium and you have time to continuously prune, staking offers good results. You can space the plants eighteen inches apart in rows three feet apart. The fruit will be very easy to find, it will be clean, and if you go easy on the pruning, you won't have trouble with splits and scalds. The fruit will also mature more than a week earlier than sprawls because of the extra sunlight hitting the plants. Staking is also the most efficient use of space. If you figure that a plot twelve by twelve feet will hold sixteen sprawl plants or forty-five staked plants, and that the sprawls bear twice as much fruit as the staked, you find that you still have one-third more production from the staked plants. I think the actual gain is far more than this. Naturally you will have to do a lot more work for that extra production in staking and pruning.

I stake this way: Before I set the plants in the field I drive two-by-two's seven feet long into the soil. The dimensions don't have to be exact. I put the plants about three inches from the stakes, and when they grow about twelve inches high I remove all but the main stem, and tie it loosely to the stake with a piece of sisal twine. As the plants grow I remove all the suckers that develop between the main stem and the leaves *below the first fruit cluster*. These suckers come out right from the stem. *Above the first fruit cluster* I allow the suckers to develop two sets of leaves, and then prune. After every twelve to fifteen inches of main-stem growth I again tie the plant to the stake. This method gives a very compact, erect plant, yet one that has some leaf to it. The trouble is—as with all pruning systems—that the job is never over. Every week I have to go through the rows and prune away all new sucker growth, and it springs up both along the new parts of the main stem and where I've already pruned. Also, if the leaves curl as if diseased when you prune or tie to stakes, wait a couple of days before searching out a cause. Tomatoes often show these symptoms as a stress reaction to these procedures and will rapidly recover. Personally I think staking, whether using trellis or stakes, is a lot of work and is worthwhile only where space is at a premium and high production is wanted.

Of course, with either staking or sprawling it's possible to plant rather than transplant. Do it about the same time as you plant corn. Plant three to five seeds in each permanent location and thin to the best one. These plants will develop extensive root systems, diving five feet deep and more, and will be stronger growers and outproduce most transplants. Their only disadvantage is that they'll begin providing a harvest two or three weeks later than transplants of the same variety.

Where there's a cutworm problem I fashion a collar out of cardboard, slip it around the tomato, staple, and press into the soil. Keep the ground moist until the plants "take," then mulch, and whenever the soil begins to dry out water again deeply. Tomatoes need a lot of water but not a soaking. If the ground does ever become dried out it's better to water a little over a period of several days than a lot all at once because the fruits may crack or split if subjected to a sudden glut of water.

As far as cold protection goes, there are various types of hot caps on the market. You can set them over transplants as you place them in the field, or you can use them just on cold nights. You can also build a plastic pup tent-like structure over the rows. I first saw these in Mexico, and they looked like long, inverted Vs. They can be closed off at either end to make a kind of cold frame. The most elaborate system I ever saw was the one devised by my neighbor whose crops were subject to killing frosts in July. He bought fiberglass panels and fashioned them into circles with the plants inside. A second piece of fiberglass went over the top. Such an individual cold frame easily goes around a mature plant and extends its bearing period a couple weeks beyond the first frost in most years.

About six weeks before you expect the first killing frost begin removing flowers as they appear. It takes thirty-five to forty-five days for a tomato to reach the green mature stage, so any tomatoes that you allow to set after the six weeks before killing frost date will go to waste. It's also a good idea to remove the terminal buds of the major vines (one for staked plants, three for nonstaked in most cases) and keep them pruned. This will help direct all new growth into producing large, mature fruit before the end of the season. To continue a harvest after a frost it's necessary to pick the unripe tomatoes before they've been touched by cold.

My friend Max, who learned a lot of cold weather tricks in his native Finland, devised a labor-intensive way to market his crop into February when he lived just across the Washington border in Canada. He said, "I listened to the weather forecasts on the radio, and when they predicted the first frost my family went into the field and picked every tomato. It took us nearly all night, but we didn't lose any to frost. We sold the red ones immediately. I saved the pink ones until they were nearly ripe, and then sold them to a local market. The manager asked me if I had a greenhouse. The tomatoes were so nice compared to the ones coming up from the southern United States."

The hardest work, he told me, was wrapping all the mature green tomatoes in newspaper and sorting them according to their degree of pinkness. Max stored them all in a basement rack. "I went through them every week. I sold the pink ones to the market, and rewrapped the rest. In February a man saw the Tomatoes for Sale sign in our front yard. It was almost covered with snow. He thought it was a joke or a gimmick so he came up to the house to see what it was all about. I went down to the basement and got him a couple pounds of nearly ripe tomatoes. He could hardly believe it. He thought I had grow-lamps and a greenhouse down there. The tomatoes were a little mushy and not full-flavored, but they were red and ripe. I think they tasted better than the ones that come from southern California and Mexico."

The more standard method of keeping tomatoes is to put them in a sunny, frost-protected place, and allow them to ripen at a faster rate. A sunny window or a hot frame are good locations and yield a better-tasting fruit than those that mature in the dark of a cellar. I think a combination of both methods would be the ideal way to extend the fresh season.

It's also possible to grow tomatoes all year around. Simply start the plants in midsummer, doing all the transplanting operations, but set them out in the greenhouse or in five-gallon containers. I feed my indoor plants regularly with a fish emulsion fertilizer, plus a teaspoon of bone meal every month. Given a sunny location where the temperature doesn't drop below 50° at night the plants will do well. Besides this method you can take twelve-inch sucker cuttings in early August, bury them up to the last couple of leaves in a rich soil or compost, and keep them well watered. They will root and then grow, producing during the winter. A variation on this is to sow seeds in flats in late December or January, and about the time you would normally be starting seeds to transplant outdoors, cut suckers from these leggy seedlings and root them as I've just described. Set them out after the ground warms up and these plants will mature fruit earlier than regular transplants.

Peppers

Gertrude Stein once said, "A rose is a rose is a rose." I wish I could make that statement about peppers, but there are so many varieties of these vegetables that it's fairly mind-boggling. To make matters worse, garden peppers are in no way related to the peppers that supply us with the common ground black and white table pepper. Garden peppers, whether they're big green bells or bitingly hot tabascos, are members of the nightshade family and are more closely related to tomatoes and potatoes than they are to black peppers. I don't know how to arrange them except to say that botanists classify them into four or six different categories. They are the cherry peppers, the cone peppers which I think includes the Tabasco, the bell peppers like our fresh-eating green peppers, and the long peppers including the cayenne, pimientos, and paprika. I think the simplest thing to say is that there are sweet peppers and hot peppers and that the two categories overlap.

Peppers will grow on just about any kind of soil, though the sandy loams are best where seasons are short or cool because they warm up faster and remain hot longer than clays or silts. Peppers need more average heat than tomatoes, but I've successfully grown them at the edge of the cool fog zone. I did notice that while my peppers had all the desirable characteristics of those grown in hotter areas they only grew to half the size. Optimum temperature for the bells is 70° to 75°, and for hot peppers, 70° to 85°. For successful outdoor germination they need a soil temperature of 60° as compared to 50° for tomatoes and corn. Once established on well-drained ground their root systems will reach down four feet and more, and will thrive in pH 5.5 to 6.5.

I handle them the way I do tomatoes for the most part. One difference is that they should have five to ten degrees more heat in the hot frame or greenhouse if possible. I also give them a side-dressing of a half-pound of bloodmeal, two pounds of bone meal, and one pound of unleached wood ashes for each fifty-five to sixty plants about two weeks after setting them out. I cultivate at the same time and add a light mulch. When I transplant I don't prune, but I do set the plants deeper than they were in the flats or pots, burying them to within an inch of the bottom leaves. As with all transplanted crops I feel that transplanting out of flats into peat pots and setting the peat pots in the soil so they're completely covered is the best way to insure vigorous, unchecked growth.

(While on the subject of peat pots, I want to caution you to make certain the tops of the pots are never level with the soil or the exposed fiber will act as a wick to draw water out of the pot and surrounding soil into the air, and the plants will not thrive. The lips of the pots must be buried under soil. Both the pot and the soil it's going into must be very moist and you should take care to keep them that way at least two weeks until the roots can push out into the soil. My second choice after peat pots for transplanting is tin cans with removable bottoms. I make mine by cutting out the bottom, and then I bend the bottom edge inward with a pliers in three places and reinsert the bottom lid. It won't fall through, but it can be pushed up and out of the container with the rooted plant ball and placed intact in the rows. There will be hardly any setback and the cost will be nil.)

I space peppers in the field at eighteen inches apart in rows two feet apart. The sweet varieties I grow are Yolo Wonder, a mosaic-resistant type that puts out a lot of protective foliage for the fruits; and California Wonder, perhaps the meatiest pepper, but a little later than the former. Hot peppers I enjoy are Long Red Cayenne, Hungarian Yellow Wax, Tabasco, and Jalepeño. The last makes an excellent pickle—green or red—with sliced carrots and cut-up bits of cauliflower. Where the season is short I suggest the Hungarian or Cayenne, as they mature in sixty-six to seventy days. That's up to a month before Tabasco. There are also pimientos that are used in stuffed olives and the paprikas. The paprika sold as a spice in markets is from a Hungarian strain of hot peppers. The hot variety is made from the whole ground pods, but the mild spice we use on egg dishes, for instance, is called rosenpaprika. It's made from pods that have had the stalks, stems, and seeded centers removed.

The sweet peppers are mild whether they're picked green-mature or red-mature. The green ones are crispier, but the reds are sweeter and have more vitamin C. I pick them any time after they're full size. The color is a deep green that has a shine and depth to it. After you've seen a few go from an immature green to a mature green you'll be able to tell. The red ones should be a deep, bright red. The greens cling tenaciously to the stems and it's best to harvest by cutting off an inch of stem with a scissors to avoid damaging the plant.

I was never a pepper eater until my first visit to Mexico about twelve years ago. Every meal the cook offered me *salsa picante* (hot sauce) and *salsa verde* (a green, mild sauce). "Eat," she invariably intoned. "What is food without chile?" I think she was apprehensive that her student charge would fall sick without a daily dose.

Eventually, to be polite, I ate some of the green sauce. I felt like one of those cartoon characters with steam coming out of his ears, but at least I learned that the hot types are hot green, and they get hotter as they turn red, purple, brown, yellow, or whatever color they're going to turn.

Later, in San Blas, my friend Jesus Sanchez gave me a few pointers on handling them. "The chiles come off easier than what you Americans call bell peppers. Sometimes they fall off. My people don't wait for them to get red. We start eating them as soon as they're full-size green. The ones that dry on the vine—muy bravo."

"Bravo," I found through hot experience, was a strong pepper. Some Central American types get so "muy mucho bravo" that even a dedicated chile lover will grimace and cry with a slight nibble. So why do people eat such food?

"Para la salud," Jesus said. "For the health. The bugs don't live where the peppers live. You eat the peppers and the bugs stay out of you. We preserve our food with pepper, and we preserve ourselves with pepper. It makes food taste better. What could be simpler?"

My wife, who packs powdered cayenne into gelatin caps and swallows them, says chiles stimulate digestion and circulation, tone the body—and like Jesus—believes they control harmful gastrointestinal bacteria. You can take it from me, a man raised in his youth on a bland Midwestern meat-and-potatoes diet, you can train yourself to enjoy peppers.

To preserve dried peppers I harvest just before the first big rainstorm of the season (elsewhere that would be before the first frost), and follow Jesus' wife Maria's plan. Whatever she's not going to use in the near future she strings with a needle and thread and hangs in an out-of-the-way corner of the kitchen. They'll get dusty, but they'll last for years if necessary. What she needs for immediate use she runs through a hand grain mill just enough to break up some of the seeds. The "flakes" turn up in all kinds of dishes. For chile powder she grinds the peppers into a fine powder, adding to it comino (cumin), tumeric, and whatever else strikes her fancy.

Even if you're not a chile eater, you ought to grow cayenne peppers for use in homemade garden sprays. Grind up three or four pods, add a couple ground cloves of garlic, a half-capful of liquid soap (not detergent) as a sticking agent, and a quart of warm water. Mix all ingredients well and let set overnight. Strain and use as a spray for ants, some maggots, caterpillars, and several other pests. This spray will also control some viruses like ringspot and cucumber mosaic. The latter, curiously enough, is one of the diseases that attacks peppers. There are a host of other sprays you can make, combining hot peppers with yarrow, stinging nettle, wormwood, sage, and other repellant heros. The pepper is ripe for experimentation in the field of natural plant pesticides and repellants.

Melons

 As a gardener with a year-around cool season I find growing melons is no easy matter, but it is worth the effort. In comparison to the melons picked unripe for long-distance shipping (most of which are selected as much for their packing and shipping qualities as for their eating merits) a homegrown early melon is far superior.

One reason that's true is that immaturely picked melons cease to manufacture sugar. They will get softer and perhaps develop a little more aroma, but that's all. Furthermore, most melons picked at their prime are best to eat right then and there. They will almost immediately begin to lose some of their sugar and firm flesh. There's no way that a store-bought melon can compare with a homegrown one unless you're buying at a roadside market from the grower. The homegrown, organic melon that is ripened on the vine, picked at maturity, and eaten as soon as possible is without com-
210

parison. I will have to admit, however, that the varieties gardeners in cool areas or with short seasons have to grow are not to be compared with those that mature over long seasons and in hot climates. The old-time, extra-sweet watermelons like Ice Cream and Sweetheart or the better homegrown muskmelons like Hale's Best, Hearts of Gold, and Honey Rock need a long time in the field and hot weather. They're indisputably superior, and should be planted where conditions permit. I have to settle for the early maturing and midget varieties, which like their counterparts among most all types of vegetables, are good but not as good as main-season varieties. But good is better than the average or so-so melons available at the market.

The melons come from two different genera of the cucumber family. The canteloupes (muskmelons), honeydews, casabas, Chinese winter melons, and mango melons are all varieties of the species *cucumis melo*, and are closely related to the cucumber. The watermelon and citron are *citrullus vulgaris*. There's not much difference among the species in culture and care. It used to be that canteloupes would grow a little farther north than watermelons, but recent introductions of early maturing strains have changed that. The watermelons, except for the dwarf varieties, require more growing space, and they tolerate pH 5.0 to 6.5 as compared to canteloupe and cucumbers that prefer a pH 6 to 7. In this chapter I'm going to discuss the melons, but cucumber culture is close. The main difference is that there's no need to disbud cucumbers before frosts because they mature so fast. Also, cucumbers should be picked as they ripen or else the vines will cease production and the fruit that is already there will get bitter.

My favorite cool weather muskmelons are Far North, a netted salmon-colored variety that matures in 65 days under ideal conditions but which has taken 100 days in my garden; Minnesota Midget, a 65-day type that has small orange fruits on compact vines; and Midget

211

Bush, a type that matures in two months. The only honey-dew I know that will mature in a short or cool season is Kazakh (70 days), and it's a dandy with a flavor as good as any market melon. Incidentally, muskmelons and canteloupes are interchangeable names in the United States, but I personally like to call the salmon- or orange-fleshed fruits canteloupes and the green-fleshed ones muskmelons. Honeydews and casabas are entirely different fruits from canteloupes and muskmelons though the line often blurs.

My choice in watermelons includes New Hampshire Midget. It yields five-pound fruits in under seventy days under ideal conditions. Golden Midget (sixty-five days) is a curiosity because its green rind turns yellow at maturity. Early Canada (seventy-five days) is a large ten- to fifteen-pound melon that I find more reliable than any other in its size range. The larger melons are out of the question for me. I have a long growing season but much of it is in the cool time of the year. Melons need hot weather as the fruits are developing. They need 70° *nights* to develop their full sugar. That means where the season extends into the fall matura-tion is all but impossible in the field without artificial means because the nights are very cool no matter how warm the day temperatures.

Starting melons indoors for future use outside is precarious business at best. I successfully do it with three-inch peat pots. I start in late March and set out plants by the beginning of May. Elsewhere it would probably be best to start seed about a month before it's time to set out tomatoes in the field. If you start them too early melons will get leggy and develop root systems too big for their containers. They do have strong root sys-tems. The watermelon will go six or more feet deep, so it's nothing for the roots to penetrate a peat pot if kept indoors too long. I give my plants a special potting mixture of two parts sharp sand, two parts good loam, two parts leaf mold or peat moss, and four parts sifted

compost to which I add one five-inch clay pot full of
bone meal per bushel basket or box. I try to give them a
warm environment. The normal hothouse temperature
commercial growers use is 80° to 85° during the day and
70° at night, but they will grow alright where tomato
transplants prosper.

With the above soil mix and temperatures you can
sow watermelons directly in a greenhouse soil at least
six inches deep and keep them there through the entire
season if you keep the vines close to the glass and
support the fruit in nets. Some friends devised a
greenhouse suitable for summer canteloupes and midget
watermelons by excavating walkways three feet deep in
the earth, raising beds six inches above the ground level,
and covering with a removable roof. The result is a
greenhouse hardly higher above the surface than the
normal cold frame. It's easy to roll up the plastic when
the warm part of the summer comes, and to replace it
when cool weather returns. When the weather is bad or
the nights cool a simple thermostat controls heating coils
and lights. This is by far the best and most economical
arrangement I've seen for indoor/outdoor growing—
combining the best of both. The plants have access to the
special soil mixture and the earth below it. For muskmelons it's imperative to keep the humidity down;
watermelons will thrive in humid conditions, but there
is the danger of mildew and fungus disease. I want to
point out that this method is not an overwinter way to
grow melons. That's a special branch of horticulture
requiring different techniques and forcing varieties of
canteloupes.

If your object is to grow plants to set outdoors,
prepare the outdoor bed by spreading two inches of
compost over the entire area. If the pH is below 6, add
a half-pound to a pound of limestone per ten square feet
for canteloupes only. If possible the melons should
follow a clover crop or some other deep subsoiler like
rape. The midget varieties need about four feet in all

directions; the larger melons, up to eight feet. The best guide is personal experience. After the initial composting I go through the patch again mixing a half-bucket of compost and a half-cup of rock phosphate for the midget, and a full bucket for the larger types, into the planting hole. The day before I set out the plants, I thoroughly irrigate the holes. The following day, I plant the melons, making sure the peat pots are covered by soil. Then I irrigate the entire plot. The ideal ground is a sandy loam with a south exposure, but I've planted in clay on a west slope by incorporating huge amounts of leaf mold and rotted mulch into the plot to make it loose and warm, and by sheltering it with windbreaks. On occasion I sow directly into the ground by first sprouting seed in moist towels. An ounce of seed should plant fifty hills. When the roots push through the seed coating I place them an inch deep, six to the hill, and later thin to the best two. Collars are a good source of protection where cutworms cause problems.

When I lived in Hawaii, store-bought watermelons were an expensive luxury, and I depended on my friend Kimo's expertise for an adequate supply. He didn't have to bother with the nuances of indoor sowing, but his outside work is worth following anywhere.

He told me, "I do a lot of hoeing at first to keep the weeds down. If they get a start it's almost impossible to get rid of them. The way I look at it, the thing that separates me from the other growers is hand work and lots of it. You only get a few old pakes (Chinese) or Filipinos nowadays who do the handwork. Everybody else thinks he can make more money with a tractor and implements. On big acreage maybe that's true, but with a small field . . . I stick to handwork."

The best tip I picked up from him was flower disbudding. "As soon as the flowers come I pinch out all the lead runners," he explained. "They only throw male flowers. I get more lateral runners this way, and the fruit grows on them. That means I get more fruit and earlier fruit. When you have land as valuable as it is here you can't afford to take up space with vines that don't produce."

I suggested that maybe he gets such good results because plants have an internal reason to quickly reproduce themselves when something threatens the normal process—like pinching. They produce more fruit with less seed, but the seed there is, is well encased in thick flesh. This is ideal for melons.

"You know, I think that's right. This old pake told me a long time ago to save my seed for five years before I use it. I never tried it but maybe it works."

The idea interested me, but all I could figure was that the longer you held seed the less viable it was. The lettuce growers in California's Salinas Valley, for example, go to the length of treating their seed to break a dormancy factor so they can plant within a few weeks after harvesting the seed. It seemed a disadvantage to save seed over a long period.

"This old pake was pretty akamai (smart)," Kimo replied. "He said the seed starts to lose life. If you keep it for five, or even ten years, the ones that do sprout will give melons with more flesh and less seed. Now that I think back on it he did have the best melons." He paused for a moment before continuing tongue in cheek, "That is, until I started in."

Determining when a watermelon is ripe is no easy task. I come from a family of watermelon eaters and I still have difficulty picking out a ripe one. I do know that if I tap on the melon and the sound comes back "think" I know I should think about another melon. If it comes back "thump" it's ripe. Mostly, though, I rely on trial and error to determine the first ripe fruits of a given variety. Once I established the "thump," color of the rind, and creamy and rough aspects of the bottom of each variety I have no trouble telling the ripe ones from the unripe. The bottoms of the fruits get creamier colored and more rough as maturity approaches. When I think the first melon is ripe I "plug" it. I take a very thin sharp knife and cut an inch-square plug about three inches deep into the melon and pull it out. I can see and taste the quality of the flesh. If it's not ready I replace the plug and try again in a few days.

Ripe muskmelons are somewhat easier to spot. They show a yellowing skin, a softness at the blossom end, and a net that is so soft you can rub it off with your hand. At this point the stem connected to the fruit should slip off at the slightest pressure. There are a few types that don't slip the stems readily, so you'll have to rely on the other signs. A few trials will give you the right timing.

Squash

 Squashes and pumpkins, no matter what the textbooks say, not only thrive in cool climates, but produce an abundant supply of wholesome food that will last from autumn to spring. I first became aware of this fact while living near the the famous globe artichoke and brussels sprouts district of central coastal California. In fields adjacent to beautiful stands of artichokes there were equally beautiful stands of field pumpkins despite the cold ocean winds and summer fog.

Later, when I moved to within a couple of miles of the ocean in northern California I grew some of the sweetest, largest squashes of my life. Big Guatemalan Blue squash, though they matured late, were deliciously sweet and tender-fleshed. The acorns produced prolifically, and so did the pumpkins. When I moved even further north to a bluff above the ocean I planted squash again, not knowing what to expect. The results: spectacular vegetables with field-sown seed in a climate where three days of 75° weather is a heat wave. Squash will thrive even where the average monthly temperature hardly goes over 50°, though maturity dates will be lengthened. I don't know why this hardiness is so because squash definitely is a hot weather crop. But I capitalize on the quirk that makes it a good cool weather bearer by making it one of our dietary staples, ranking it in importance with peas, beans, corn, and tomatoes. Each cup provides 130 calories, four grams of protein, more than 8,000 units of vitamin A, and varying percentages of other vital vitamins and minerals.

When I speak of squashes in this chapter I'm also speaking of pumpkins, but I'm excluding summer squash. Winter squash and pumpkins are of identical culture. The summer squash requires somewhat different handling from the other two, though it is in fact a pumpkin, and not a squash. The summer squash is a compact, bushy plant that yields heavily from mid-season until frost kills the plants. It deserves a space in every garden because one or two plants will supply a family's fresh needs for several months.

Summer squash culture is easy. Either start in peat pots as with melons or sow in the ground after it has warmed up. I plant five seeds to the hill and thin to the best two. Proper depth of planting is one inch, and the plants should be spaced three feet in every direction. I've found that for cool weather climates the black zucchini is the best of the cocozelle varieties. Among the other types early prolific straight or crookneck, and white and green patty pans do well, but not as well as zucchini.

The long squashes should be picked before they're six inches long, and the patty pans when they're about three inches in diameter. Beyond these points the fruits get tough and the flavor drops off appreciably. I pick the fruit whether I plan on eating it or not because production will cease if plants are allowed to remain on the vines. If you plan on processing the squash for bread and butter pickles, or for frozen vegetables, you can figure that 100 feet of row will yield 200 pounds of fruit, and that each quart—canned or frozen—requires 2 to 3 pounds of fresh vegetables. One ounce of seed will plant twenty to forty hills, depending on the variety and rate of seeding.

By the way, now that a couple of the big English seed companies are selling on the American market, don't get confused over the terms cocozelle and marrow squashes. The first time I ate cocozelle, my hostess, a young woman of Italian descent, served me zucchinis about five inches long stuffed with tomatoes, melted Monterrey jack cheese, and spices. Sometime later, after I moved to the Whitethorn area, I partook of a very large squash that had been chopped into a soup. The hostess in this case was English and she told me the squash was a marrow. In both cases I would have called the vegetable a zucchini. The English are fond of eating their zucchinis full-grown and insipid (my bias), and calling them marrows. The Italians cook them young and tender, and often prefer a particular variety called cocozelle. I hope that clears up the nomenclature. As for me, black zucchini is tops.

Winter squashes and pumpkins are much different from summer squash, perhaps the most outstanding difference being that it's possible to space the latter two feet by two feet, whereas I've spaced Hubbards at eight by ten feet and they crowded each other in the end. If anything, winter squashes should be handled much like melons. They don't need any summer greenhouse treatment because they withstand cool weather better, but it is a good idea to start them indoors in peat pots. I never prune the vines except to remove the fruit flowers that appear after August 1. In fact I don't do much of anything to this crop but water once they're established. They like a pH 5.5 to 6.5, a rich soil, and a deep mulch or partial shade. They'll grow as well on clay as on a sand loam. I prefer to grow them between corn or sunflowers, but if you set them out in the field they should be spaced a minimum of four by six feet for the smaller types, and six by six for the Hubbards and pumpkins. An ounce of seed should plant a hundred feet of row that yields 400 or more pounds of squash.

To grow among corn I allow eight feet by ten feet for all varieties. I let the corn get about six inches high before putting in squash and pumpkin transplants. This works out well because the ground is a little too cool for squashes when I sow corn, and there's a possibility of the former getting stunted. If I sowed seed at the time I sow corn it would surely rot in the ground. The two crops get along well together. The squashes provide a cool living mulch for the corn and the corn shades the squashes from the direct rays of the sun, and of course I get two crops from one space. For my plantings at the seashore I plant the squash in its own beds because the climate is naturally fog-shaded.

Where space is at a premium you can train squashes to climb walls or trellises if you hang the fruit in mesh or cloth nets. They are strong enough that you don't have to use supports, but from my own experiences with vertical planting I've come to the conclusion that a twenty-pound fruit hanging unsupported causes an undue strain on the plant. All the energy it uses to form strong supportive stems should go into fruit production.

For winter keepers it's imperative that you handle the fruit properly. I divide mine into three categories. The first is the group that matured a month or more before the first big rainstorm of the season (or frost, if that's the case). The second is the group that matured between a month before and the end of the season. The third group includes those that didn't mature. The last group I use as soon as possible in soups and stews because it won't last long at all, and the quality isn't very good. The middle group I use up first in the winter, and save the earliest maturers for late-winter eating and for seed. With some varieties these last-to-be-eaten squash will have a high vitamin A content and more sugar than if you used them at first. It's important that squashes be protected from all frosts. If frost touches the plants the fruit will rot quickly. I harvest by cutting off an inch of stem to use as a handle. I also avoid bruising the fruit in the least as a bruised fruit is sure to rot. Ideally I like to subject the squash to 80° to 90° temperature in a well-ventilated, dry atmosphere for about a week, but often this is impossible because there are so many other vegetables and herbs drying at the end of the season. Where the sun is hot during the day this curing occurs right in the field and makes a tough dry skin. If I'm not able to provide the necessary heat I store them in single layers as near as possible to temperatures between 50° and 55° in as dry a room as possible. I go through the storage shelves every couple weeks and sort out the soft ones for first use.

I only plant a few varieties nowadays because through experimentation I've found they produce well and last a long time in my climate with no special tricks of the trade. Acorn (Des Moines or Table Queen) and the Chicago Green and Blue Hubbards are the ones I depend on. The acorns are best eaten at the beginning of the season because they don't last as long as the Hubbards. If I lived in a normal climate (one with no summer fog) I would definitely plant Guatemala Blue, which I consider the king of the squashes for flavor and texture. My next choices are a tie between Butternut and Buttercup, both of which have excellent flavor and keeping qualities.

I used to plant pumpkins in quantity, but they are not long keepers, and the Hubbards make a better pumpkin pie any day. It always seemed when I planted pumpkins the pigs were the greatest beneficiaries of the crop. Now if I plant them at all I stick to Sugar Pie, Connecticut Field, and Winter Keeper (the best keeper). Sugar Pie is the tastiest and Connecticut, a dependable big yielder. There is a certain demand for them for pies and for autumn decorations that the other squashes don't meet.

14
Long Season Root Crops

Whether based on ethnic background, taste, availability, or cost we all have our vegetable preferences. Among the root crops I have a preference for the two long-season crops—parsnips and salsify—for a variety of reasons.

Growing—and Eating—Parsnips

Fresh, hot buttered parsnips garnished with parsley is one of those Thanksgiving and Christmas delights that goes back to my boyhood. Years later, during the first winter of my back-to-the-land experience I had just enough money to pay the mortgage (sometimes) and maybe twenty dollars a month for food. Parsnips happened to be one of the few vegetables I could buy cheaply and organically so I became adept at eating baked, broiled, fried, mashed, and scalloped parsnips.

When I began planting my own crops I found that parsnips thrived in the cool coastal climate, developing huge roots that went down two feet—certainly an economical use of my then limited growing soil. They were also completely winter-hardy, and I could store them in the ground. A freeze doesn't bother them at all (alternate thaws and freezes do, however, so they should be protected from such conditions by a mulch). The best part was that at a time of year when most crops had passed their prime the parsnips were just coming in. The root starches change to sugars after a series of light frosts, and the flavor fairly blooms in cold weather. Across the board, in protein, vitamins, and minerals, parsnips compare favorably with the potato, and compared to carrots, beets, or turnips, they're the very height of nutrition.

Along the north coast I plant parsnips (and this goes for salsify, also) in June because the growing season is very long and very slow and the first frosts won't come until December. Elsewhere they probably should be planted about May 1. They take about four months to mature, so I place them in an out-of-the-way spot where their presence for the next eight or nine months won't interfere with other gardening operations.

The parsnip is a very large, deep-rooted vegetable. Given a loose soil, deeply prepared and well fertilized with a two-inch layer of compost, and a sprinkling of two-thirds rock phosphate and one-third wood ashes at the rate of one pound per fifty square feet, the parsnip will grow four inches in diameter at the shoulder and be as large at a depth of twelve inches as a Chatenay carrot is at the soil surface. The root system goes down well past the four-foot mark. I try to loosen the soil at least a foot deep (I don't actually turn the topsoil twelve inches, but spade the first six inches, and then push the spade as far as it will go in the loose soil and wiggle it back and forth). Sometimes I use a mattock to loosen the soil. Another alternative is to follow a crop like rape or Swiss chard.

A quarter-ounce of seed will sow a fifty-foot row, but make sure the seed is fresh. Even under good conditions viability is only a year or two. I make my rows fifteen inches wide, and sow the seed sparingly in the rows a half-inch deep. Parsnips are very hard to germinate and weak growers besides. That was a hard lesson I learned when almost a whole June planting failed to break the surface one year, and that was on ground I thought I had kept loose and moist. Apparently there was just a slight crust, and I had sowed a little too deeply. After the parsnips germinated they pushed up to the crust, and turned and went parallel to the surface until they exhausted themselves and died.

There was time to replant and the ever-innovative Tom Becotte had an idea. "Let's do with them what we do with the parsley."

I tried to recall what it was that we did with parsley that would work with parsnips.

"Sow radishes in the rows," Tom insisted.

It was a splendid idea. Radishes—dropped sparingly in the rows—have vigorous sprouts that break through crusts or compensate for deeply sown weaker seeds, and push the soil surface up so that parsnips can follow through to the sunlight. (Even if there is no crust the seeds will be up quicker with the radishes than by themselves. With a radish like Radar that matures in eighteen days there's no danger of the radishes blocking the needs of the parsnips. The radishes marking the row before the parsnips germinate also provide a convenient guide for weeding operations.)

When the parsnips are four to five inches high thin them to stand about four inches in the row. I thin on time because the rootlets and taproots can get terribly mixed up, and if you pull one you'll damage two others when you thin late. When I cultivate I also mulch, and except for watering whenever the soil surface dries out, parsnips need no further attention until harvest.

Salsify: The Oyster Plant

My second long season root crop—salsify—is one I had never heard of until I became an organic gardener. A neighbor told me about it, claiming it had a flavor reminiscent of oysters, hence its alternate name, oyster plant. The possibility of a vegetable that could add an ocean flavor to my diet intrigued me and I planted the two kinds of salsify I could find. One was the white salsify, Mammoth

Sandwich Islands, which is closely allied to chicory; the other was black salsify, or scorzonera. As it turned out both roots had a texture somewhat like parsnips, and could be cooked in the same way. They also did smell and taste a little like oysters and the white has an edible stalk that can be used like asparagus when it comes up the second year. I acquired a liking for both of them, although to my taste buds the black is tops. It has a more pronounced oyster flavor as well as a grainy texture I find appealing. Breaded and fried like oysters, it's a real treat. If you're not already a fan of these two vegetables I suggest you follow my planting instructions, limiting yourself to ten feet of row for each as a trial. They're definitely "I like them. Let's plant some more," or "Don't ever waste space on that stuff again" vegetables.

The salsify isn't as deep-rooted, and is more like a large carrot in size, but it likes basically the same treatment as parsnips. One difference between the two is in seeding. Salsify is a strong grower and with fresh seed you'll have no trouble getting a good stand. Just be careful when weeding as young plants look like grass. In fact, for years I had planned to try this crop to see if the "oyster" claims were true but for one reason or another, I always forgot. Eventually I planted a couple packets. They were well up and looking good and my wife and I were anticipating our first taste of salsify. Meanwhile a friend visited us and asked if he could help in the garden. He "weeded" the salsify. After all, they looked like unwanted blades of grass to him.

Salsify, like parsnips, will stand all winter in the rows, but it must be used up before growth starts in the spring. Both parsnip and salsify roots quickly deteriorate as vegetables as the plant uses its vital stored energy to produce a seed stalk. Of course, if you like this cold weather duo as well as I do, they'll be long gone before the time growth should resume.

224

15
When Winter's Around the Corner

The winter garden is the most complicated uncomplicated gardening subject I know. Basically, it's a section or sections of the garden that are planted between the first of July and the first of September so crops will ripen in late fall for use throughout the winter and early spring. Though this sounds uncomplicated there are some things which must be dealt with if the garden is to be successful as, for instance, the first frost dates, how to use cover crops and green manures, the suitability of vegetable varieties, days to maturity, mulches, additional fertilizing, frost protection, and harvesting.

My winter garden is always a tentative proposition. True, I always set aside a winter portion when I make my general garden plan. It's usually a section with a valuable cover crop on it from the previous fall that will be turned under and given a chance to decompose before the ground is worked up for a crop. But the big factors in deciding whether or not this will become the winter garden are the weather and succession plantings. For example, I may plan to follow early corn with carrots, but then the first corn gets wiped out by bad weather. I plant again and the weather remains cold and the stand gets off to a very slow start. Instead of being ready in early July the corn is ready in early August. Experience has taught me that if I plant carrots in early August they will go into the winter half grown and will not develop their full flavor or size. So I alter the plan and sow fall radishes.

If you have a small garden you might not want to leave a portion of it fallow or under cover until July, but would rather depend entirely on succession crops. In such cases the first thing I take into account is the lay of the land. The light soils that warm up fastest in spring and have the most exposures (such as a south slope or an area near a south wall or fence) are also the plots that resist cold weather longest in fall. Heavy clays, west and north slopes, terrain exposed to winds, hollows, and depressions are all the places frost bites first. The first frost of the season usually comes rather unexpectedly and is often followed by a couple of weeks of very warm weather that we call Indian Summer. This means that if you afford tender plants protection from the first frost you can extend your harvest into the fall. Planning protection for a few tomatoes and peppers should be considered part of the winter garden.

All vegetables other than tender ones (like peppers, melons, or eggplant) fall into three categories. The first is the entirely hardy plants, including broccoli, brussels sprouts, kale, spinach, leek, parsnips, and salsify. I grow the first five year-around. I time the two roots crops so they're ready to harvest by mid-October, but then I allow them to remain in their rows until needed. In areas where the ground freezes all these crops will need some protection—the roots with mulch to prevent them from going through alternate freezes and thaws, and the leafy types with mulch as well as some kind of protection that gives them heat to grow. "Entirely hardy" means plants will stand through a freezing winter and resume growth in spring. It does not mean they will continue to grow through a freezing winter unless you provide protection.

The second group is the hardy plants, including carrots, onions, lettuce, peas, and rutabagas. Again, these crops will go through heavy frosts, but should be harvested before the ground freezes. Where the ground doesn't freeze they will stand in rows all winter. Frozen lettuce must be thawed slowly in cold water and used immediately.

The third group is the half-hardy plants. They will also stand and even grow with minimal protection in mild climates. They include beets, cabbage, cauliflower, celery, Chinese cabbage, radishes, and chard. You can't expect them to stand more than light frosts, so it's best to plan on harvesting them by the end of Indian Summer if you live in a cold zone. The roots like beets should be mulched deeply if you plan to store them in the rows. Along the north coast I grow all these crops all year long. Some of them don't do any more than stand in rows and wait for warm weather, but others show a very slow growth.

Frost Considerations

The object of the winter garden is to select varieties that will mature within the frost range that the plant will tolerate.* Below are some illustrations of how I handle the winter garden in my locality. I don't have to bother about frosts too much except for tender vegetables, but I've learned that short days, lack of heat, and five months of cold, hard rains limit my growing many crops just as a late October frost would.

Take corn and beans in my fall garden. Theoretically they should continue to grow until frost kills them in mid-December. In fact, I have to plan on maturing these crops by late October or they won't make it. Because of the general coolness of the summer season I select a medium-season main crop like Golden Cross Bantam (eighty-five days) and a main-crop snap bean like Kentucky Wonder (sixty-five days). By planting them both around July 1 the corn will be ready in mid-October. The beans will have been producing for a couple of weeks by then, but they will be tapering off rapidly. Had I planted a long-season corn like Country Gentleman it would never have matured because of lack

---

*There are several frost ranges. They are: light frost which severely damages tender plants; heavy frost that destroys tender crops and damages hardy ones; and killing frost that kills the staple crops in the region and means that perennials and biennials will stop growing until the next spring.

227

of heat at the end of the season; similarly a lima bean would never have made it.

Another example is carrots. When I first moved to the north coast I figured since the weather was mild I could plant carrots in September and have nice roots by the beginning of December. Not so. By March the roots were about one-third their full size and large-cored. I revised my planting schedule to late July. Theoretically the carrot would be full size by mid-October, but because of the slowness of the season, it didn't come to maturity until sometime in late November. For purposes of winter harvests this is ideal for me.

The point is to plant every species of winter vegetable so that it will mature in the last possible days of the season. To determine those times in your own garden will require paying close attention to the weather, observation, and experimentation. You can see that I plant my corn so that there's just enough heat left in the season to mature the crop in mid-October. This gives me fresh corn over a long season. On the other hand, I plant carrots so they'll mature in late November. If I tried to mature them later they wouldn't make it. If I matured them earlier they would be at their peak before I actually needed them, and because there was still some growing season left for them, they would go past their prime and develop less-than-perfect characteristics. I can time brussels sprouts and kale, however, to grow all winter as these crops won't deteriorate if they keep growing.

I think you get the idea of timing your plantings from these two illustrations, but don't let length of days to maturity (adjusted by experience to your climatic conditions) be your sole guideline. The very tender and sweet carrot Touchon, for example, does not fare well when planted in the winter garden. For some peculiar reason of its own it likes to start and complete its growth in cool spring weather. All the beets will do well in winter, but the variety Winter Keeper is particularly bred for its keeping qualities. I don't plant turnips for the

winter, but I do grow rutabagas as they're more nutritious for the cold season, and frost improves their flavor.

Planting in Late Summer

Another consideration is the cultural differences
between summer and winter gardens. The two major
difficulties in sowing or transplanting crops in July or
August are lack of water and too much heat. Both are
easy to overcome by irrigation. The reason heat causes
problems is because it dries out the soil. In such cases
seeds fail to germinate, or if they do germinate, they
wither in the hot sun. A transplant may also wilt and die
on a hot day. For unchecked growth it's necessary to
transplant into moist soil, and it's best to do it when the
heat of the day is subsiding. That will give the plant
nearly twenty hours before strong heat returns.

My suggestion is to sow large seeds (corn, chard,
beans, peas) about a half-inch deeper than you would in
spring, and the smaller seeds about a quarter-inch
deeper. It's not necessary to replow or spade the ground
in succession planting, but I always clear all the debris
from the previous crop to the compost heap. I open the
furrows and mix additional fertilizer directly into the
rows and water well. The next morning I plant. I water
again immediately, and continue to do so daily until the
seedlings are established. If you're transplanting and the
weather is unusually hot and sunny, it's often a good
idea to provide some kind of protective shade for the
plants until their root systems are able to absorb enough
water without wilting. This kind of hot weather stress
rarely happens with peat-pot or tin-can transplants. Failure to apply sufficient water is a major factor in poor
stands of winter crops. Watering with a harsh spray that
washes out seeds or causes puddling and subsequent
hardening of the surface is also a problem. Common
sense eliminates both.

Cover Crops
and the Winter Garden

Another major consideration in the winter garden is cover crops. In a small garden you might want to plant every square inch to vegetables, depending on outside sources for mulch, compost, and soil amendments. In medium and large gardens it's best to set aside a part of the winter garden for green manures. Good crops to follow with covers are heavy feeders. The main corn crop, for example, could be followed by a greens like mustard, but it's far better to put it into rape to be turned under the following spring. Onions planted the previous fall and harvested in August leave a gap that could be planted to radishes, but which would better be utilized with a cover crop. Whatever your choices, try to rotate your whole garden on some kind of systematic basis.

There are many ways to do this. One is by vegetable families; another is by trying to follow roots with fruits, followed by salad plants, followed by seeds. On a long rotation you might start with peas in the spring, followed by beets or chard that would stand until the next spring. Then you would plant the cabbage family, followed in late summer by a green manure, the next spring by corn, then winter carrots, then a summer of tomatoes, followed by peas the next spring. If the climate was a mild one you could put a winter cover like rape or rye and vetch after the tomatoes, turn it under in the spring, and go into rotation with a legume like beans instead of peas. At any rate you would be back to legumes by the fifth year. The climate and how well you plan your garden will determine the amount of time it takes to go through a rotation.

Overwinter Protection

The final consideration is protecting plants from the first few frosts so as to prolong the season, or providing some kind of overwinter protection in order to grow hardy or entirely hardy plants on a production basis. For the latter two categories the easiest solution is a cold frame or a hot frame. Your cold frame could be nothing more than a few bales of hay arranged in a rectangle with well-mulched crops within, and the whole covered by storm windows or plastic (see chapter 8). Plastic tents will help to ward off light frosts from tender plants. The elaborate fiberglass cylinders my neighbor had for his tomatoes, inverted bushel baskets or boxes, or a fine drizzle at night* are other considerations. The criterion for using these things should be: Will the covering pay for itself in increased vegetable yields, will it be usable for several seasons, and is the time expended in providing frost protection worth the return in produce.

There are some vegetables that do particularly well in the winter garden. Among these are the Chinese vegetables like michihli and bok choy and winter radishes. I'd now like to turn my attention to cultivating these.

Michihli, Chihli, Wong Bok, and Bok Choy

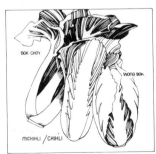

The first time I grew bok choy and wong bok everything went smoothly. I sowed the seed about the first of August, watered well, and thinned for greens when the plants were about five inches high. Going into the winter I mulched them heavily and they stood in rows eighteen inches apart, six inches from each other in the rows.

---

*It may seem difficult to believe, but a light rain may actually protect plants. If ice forms around the plant at 32°, the ice acts as insulation and the plant will then be protected against lower temperatures.

Through the whole winter and into early spring I harvested the outer leaves and an occasional head. The wong bok got rough and tough and bolted to seed in the spring before the finer-flavored and more tender bok choy, but both rewarded me a hundredfold for the care I had given them.

Encouraged by my initial success I planted that spring. Before they were half grown the plants bolted to seed. I couldn't figure it out. The weather was cool. I tried again and they bolted to seed. The following year I bought two other varieties and replanted. Again, the plants bolted to seed. Then I learned the truth about michihli, chihli, wong bok, and bok choy. They don't like long days or hot weather. The first time I planted the length of days was declining and the weather was getting cooler. The other times the temperatures were too high or the days too long. Like spinach they need either a very early cool season in which to grow, or a late cool season. Unlike spinach they are not extremely hardy. In fact they're less hardy than regular cabbages. After much frustration with transplanting early crops and having them bolt I've settled on growing these vegetables only in the fall and winter garden.

Are they worth the fuss of planting them at a certain season? Let me quote from the DiGiorgi Co., Inc. seed catalog concerning bok choy, "Resembles an immense head of lettuce, but the leaves have very prominent midribs, exceedingly tender and juicy. The hearts are most excellent to be eaten raw either as celery or with salad dressing as a salad proper. Boiled or stewed, no other greens quite equal it in tenderness and exquisite flavor. The whole plant is remarkably succulent, crisp, and tender. All who have tried baktoy [bok choy] are hearty in the praises of its flavor and high quality." The description goes on to say that bok choy can be planted in the early spring and that it will stand a long time without bolting. I find this last statement more true of bok choy than I do of the other three I've mentioned. They seem to be more temperamental, perhaps because they're actually a different species than bok choy.

All of them are brassicas, but varieties that form slender, upright heads like pe-tsai, wong bok, michihli, and chihli are specifically called *brassica pekinensis*. They are closely related to European types of cabbage. Bok choy (or paktoy or baktoy) goes under the botanical name *b. chinensis*, and is more closely allied to the mustard members of the cruciferae family. I prefer bok choy for all-around use. All of them need a rich soil well supplied with nitrogen, lots of water, and a cool season.

I feed them two inches of compost spread over the entire planting bed before sowing, plus an additional pound for every three feet of row. These plants stand close in the rows because they grow upright, but they are big and leafy. They're also shallow-rooted so there's no sense in doing more than raking the nutrients into the surface soil. Planting depth is one-half an inch. I sow very thinly—about one seed to the inch. They're quick, good germinators as long as the midsummer seedbed is moist. I thin to stand four inches apart when they're two inches tall, and thin to eight inches whenever they begin to crowd each other, usually when they're about seven inches tall. I also cultivate both these times. At the second thinning I give them a second application of fertilizer—bloodmeal at the rate of four pounds per 100 feet of row, applied in a band five inches from the plants and two inches deep. The last step is to provide a deep mulch that will help keep them warm during the frosty times ahead.

I let the plants stand all winter, harvesting the outer leaves or heads with a sharp knife as I need them. Where heavy frosts occur it's necessary to pull the Chinese cabbages, roots and all, with the soil attached and store them in a frost-proof root cellar. They will keep up to six weeks or more this way. I've never had occasion to store bok choy more than a few days under refrigeration, but it seems the leaves would last a couple of weeks under the same conditions I outlined above.

Winter Radishes

There are some members of the radish clan that transcend the humble role of catch crop and become one of the staples in the winter garden. I'm talking about winter radishes, a type unlike the ordinary radish in that it takes two months or more to mature, it grows only in late summer for autumn winter use, and often grows to prodigious size.

The biggest is Sakurajima, a Japanese variety that tips the scales at thirty pounds under optimum conditions. I've never gotten one to grow over ten pounds, but even that's a lot of radish. It has a mild flavor, and a crisp, turniplike consistency. Round Black and Long Black Spanish are two others I grow. They're excellent keepers with a slight peppery taste. The long variety—like Sakurajima—likes a deeply prepared soil, but the round type will thrive under just about any conditions. My favorite is China Rose. It's pink, about the size of a stubby carrot, and stands reliably in good condition from late fall until early spring. Lastly there's the Japanese Daikon, a long white radish that is sliced into chips and pickled as an appetizer of the same name. The China Rose also makes Daikon.

I raise all these radishes the same way. In early September I sow seed a half-inch deep in furrows fifteen inches apart. Once the plants are up I thin to six inches for the Spanish, ten inches for the Sakurajima, and four to five inches for the China Rose. The soil has to have lots of phosphorus and potassium. I use two pounds each of rock phosphate and wood ashes per 100 feet of row in addition to a one-inch layer of compost dug into the beds. I also sprinkle wood ashes on the surface around each radish to repel root maggots.

Because they're hardy, you can plant them up to sixty days before a killing frost. Mine go through light frosts all winter long and have even withstood snow blankets. In warmer areas, or protected by a cold frame, they'll grow year around for use as needed. I find it's best in the mildly cold areas such as where I live to plan for the crop to stand in the ground all winter after maturing in November. Growth will be extremely slow after that, and it won't impair the quality of the vegetable at all.

I use these radishes in soups, stews, sliced on appetizer trays, and even cut up and put on sandwiches. They're not very high in nutrients but they do contain some vitamins B, C, and a little iron and calcium. Some herbalists think the Spanish varieties are good blood purifiers, and I'm also inclined to think that their value in the diet in terms of roughage in some ways outweighs their other advantages.

THE CLEAN, ORDERLY GARDEN

Epilogue:
Cleaning Up

As the old saying goes, "Cleanliness is next to godliness." In the prosperous garden this isn't just a quaint axiom, but an absolute necessity. I've learned by hard experience that good garden management is clean garden management. There's no room for the half-done job, the slovenly job, or any other kind of job except one that is intelligently planned, well executed, and done at the right time.

Cleanliness is just as important as any other phase of gardening. In some specialized work, such as propagating plants in greenhouses, it's the thing on which every other operation hinges, and often spells the difference between profit or disasterous loss (if, for instance, a fungus like dampening-off invades the premises through lack of cleanliness). Oddly enough, just the way men laughed at the antiseptic and later aseptic approach to human and animal disease control and operating procedures, that's the way many people react to cleanliness in the garden.

Here's the careless gardener: When he gets behind a week on the weeding it takes him an additional three weeks to catch up. When he neglects an uncultivated patch he loses green manure or the crop that could have grown there and ends up with weeds to fight. The weed seeds will spread throughout the garden, and as the adage goes, "One year's weeds, seven years' seeds." Wherever debris collects he makes paths around it at an inconvenience and loss of time. These piles, besides harboring pests, have a tendency to grow and become unsightly garbage dumps. Equipment he didn't clean off and oil after use gets rusty. The wooden parts crack, warp, and weather quickly without rubdowns of linseed oil. Worse, when he doesn't put something back in its

237

proper place he wanders around sometimes for whole mornings wondering, "What did I do with that trowel. I just had it yesterday." He doesn't mend broken equipment because his attitude is, "It still works. I'll keep using it." This usually results in the need for a costly repair or new equipment. He postpones buying a needed tool, and then invariably has to halt whatever work he's doing to go and purchase it when he has to have it in the middle of a job.

I'm not exaggerating about these things. I've done each of them myself, and I've worked with scores of people in the garden, and the attitude of many has been, "This will do," or "It'll wait until tomorrow." Similarly, I have a friend, the manager of an orchard that grosses over a million dollars a year, who is meticulous in every orchard detail save one: He would rather spend hours of down time and labor on worn-out machinery than buy the new equipment that would ultimately save him much more. This kind of attitude in the garden means the sowing, cultivating, or mulching won't get done quite as well as it should be. Probably the yield will be less, or the work will have to be done over in extreme cases. Using worn-out tools generally means it will take longer to do the same job than if the right tool were used.

Cleanliness cures all these bad habits. Everything always goes back to its place immediately after use, whether a trowel or the trellises that held up the last pea crop. Each vegetable, as it matures, is harvested and the inedible remains are either composted or turned under. It's a simple matter on the daily rounds of the garden to pick up all paper and debris that have blown in. I don't allow weeds to grow except the ones I've left there for a specific purpose. I buy only good tools and maintain them well. I will buy a good secondhand tool, but never a worn one. After I use a packet of seeds I tape the open end shut and put it in a cool, dry storage place.

When I was growing up in Chicago the man who lived next to one of my cousins had a backyard business called Montclair Iris Gardens. We used to make fun of him because he was out among his flowers every morning, crawling on his hands and knees, looking at bugs with a magnifying glass, jotting down remarks in his notebook, poking sticks with identifying tags in the ground. We thought it was ludicrous that a grown man should act like that, and though I'm ashamed to admit it today (and I hope he forgives me), we sometimes switched the tags at night.

After moving to the country and getting more involved with gardening I began to appreciate what my cousin's iris-fancier neighbor was doing. In fact I came to the point that when I visited I made it a point to see what was new at the Iris Gardens. As it turned out the ludicrous neighbor had scores of prize-winning flowers to his credit, and some new strains that he had personally developed. It didn't just happen. For years he wrote down every garden operation in his journal. He didn't have to guess about what he did last week, or last year, or five years ago. To watch him go about his rounds was instruction in cleanliness and care. He removed brown and dying leaves, nursed ailing plants, checked for insects and disease, and dealt with them immediately. As each iris bloomed he noted those with outstanding characteristics and tied ribbons around the ones he wanted to save for future use. What he was doing didn't make any perceptible difference in one year, but over ten or twenty years, faithfully carried out, he developed award-winning irises.

I carried his example over into my own garden, especially in the area of seed. The field of plants I have to base my selections on is established long before harvest on the basis of vigor and conformation, and only afterwards do I add in yield, taste, and maturity date. Seed selection is not something I do at the last minute after I've already harvested and eaten the earliest, tastiest vegetables.

I've found where cleanliness and order are established habits, the work of the garden flows easily. There are peaks and lulls because of the seasonal nature of the work, but there isn't a backlog. Backlogs do not promote optimum production. To eliminate them means to take time off from the normal routine to take care of something that should have been part of the normal routine a week or a month ago. Sometimes the damage is impossible to correct. For example, peppers, tomatoes, squashes, and melons will not mature fruit set six weeks before the first expected frost. To not do a clean job of disbudding every few days will only mean immature fruit that won't be good for anything but the compost pile. Worse, the mature fruits will have lost the benefit of having growing energy channeled to them.

At the end of the season I update my journal, clean out the garden shed, service and replace worn parts in power equipment, make sure all the ground is covered with a crop, a cover, or a mulch, and that there is no vegetable residue left lying in the fields. I put all possible organic matter into the compost piles before insulating them against rains and cold weather that could slow down biological action or leach away nutrients. Lastly, I make a habit of going through my stored grains and beans on a monthly basis, and produce on a weekly basis to eliminate rotting food and to check for insect and rodent damage.

I find satisfaction and enjoyment in this work. It's a part of the very rhythm of life itself. Nature never puts off until tomorrow what it's right to do today; neither should the organic gardener. It's a hallmark of thriftiness and prosperity, and the fruit of it is health and abundance.

Bibliography

Carson, Rachel. *Silent Spring*. Boston: Houghton Mifflin Company, 1962.

Handbook on Biological Control of Plant Pests. Brooklyn, New York: Brooklyn Botanic Garden, 1960. (Available from the Brooklyn Botanic Garden, 1000 Washington Avenue, Brooklyn, New York 11225.)

Howard, Albert. *An Agricultural Testament*. New York: Oxford University Press, 1943.

Howard, Albert. *The Soil and Health*. New York: Devin-Adair Company, 1947.

Hunter, Beatrice Trum. *Gardening Without Poisons*. 2nd ed. Boston: Houghton Mifflin, 1971.

Kains, Maurice Grenville. *Making Horticulture Pay*. New York: Orange Judd, 1909.

King, Franklin Hiram. *Farmers of Forty Centuries*. Emmaus, Pennsylvania: Rodale Press, Inc., 1973.

Kirk, Donald. *Wild Edible Plants of the Western United States*. Healdsburg, California: Naturegraph Publishers, 1970.

Kloss, Jethro. *Back to Eden*. Beverly Hills, California: Woodbridge Press, 1973.

Logsdon, Gene. *The Gardener's Guide to Better Soil*. Emmaus, Pennsylvania: Rodale Press, Inc., 1975.

Lust, John. *The Herb Book*. Simi Valley, California: Benedict Lust, 1974.

Medsger, Oliver. *Edible Wild Plants*. New York: Macmillan, 1972.

Meyer, Joseph E. *The Herbalist*. rev. ed. New York: Sterling Publishing Company, Inc., 1968.

Ogden, Samuel R. *Step-by-Step to Organic Vegetable Growing*. Emmaus, Pennsylvania: Rodale Press, Inc., 1971.

Philbrick, John and Philbrick, Helen. *The Bug Book: Harmless Insect Controls*. Carlotte, Vermont: Garden Way Publishing, 1974.

Raphael, Ray. *An Everyday History of Somewhere.* New York: Alfred A. Knopf, 1974.

Robinson, Benjamin Lincoln and Fernald, Merritt Lyndon, eds. *Gray's Manual of Botany.* 7th ed. New York: American Book Company, 1908.

Rodale, J. I. *Complete Book of Composting.* Emmaus, Pennsylvania: Rodale Press, Inc., 1960.

Rodale, J. I. *How to Grow Vegetables and Fruits by the Organic Method.* Emmaus, Pennsylvania: Rodale Press, Inc., 1961.

Sims, W. L. et al. *Home Vegetable Gardening.* rev. ed. Berkeley, California: California Agricultural Extension Services, 1977.

Stout, Ruth. *How to Have a Green Thumb Without an Aching Back.* Hicksville, New York: Exposition Press, Inc., 1955.

United States Department of Agriculture. *1957 Yearbook of Agriculture, Soils.* Washington, D. C.: Government Printing Office, 1957.

Yepsen, Roger B., Jr., ed. *Organic Plant Protection.* Emmaus, Pennsylvania: Rodale Press, Inc., 1976.

Index

Index

Crop rotation, for disease control, 66

Cultivator, need in garden, 78

Cutworm, protection against, 203

D

Daikon. *See* Winter radishes

Diary, garden. *See* Journal

Disease, control of, 65–66

Dock, general growing tips for, 165

Dolomite, use to control pH of soil, 39–40

Drip irrigation, description of, 23–27

Dust, as mulch material, 60–61

E

Edible-podded peas. *See* Peas, edible-podded

Egyptian onion. *See* Onions

Emitters, in drip irrigation, 23

Endive, general growing tips for, 162

Equipment. *See* Tools

Erosion, control by cover cropping, 42

Euphorbia. *See* Gopher plant

F

Faba bean. *See* Fava beans

Fava beans, 103-8

as green manure crop, 108

harvesting, 106

inoculating, 105

presoaking to ensure germination, 104

Fennel, general growing tips for, 162–63

Fertilizers, application of, 36–39

in drip irrigation system, 23

natural sources of, 33–34

Fiberglass, use as cold frame cover, 93

use as mulch material, 61

Field capacity, of soil, 17

Field peas. *See* Peas

Fish emulsion, as fertilizer, application of, 38–39

Foxglove, as iron and manganese source for compost, 36

Frost, dealing with, in garden, 227–28

Fungus, control of, 65

G

Garlic, as companion plant, 118–19

general growing tips for, 135

Germination test, of seeds, 82

Glass wool, as mulch material, 61

Globe artichoke. *See* Artichoke, globe

Index

Index

R

Radishes, summer, 166
  watering of, 18
Radishes, winter, general
  growing tips for, 234–35
Rain. *See* Water
Raised beds, for intensive
  gardening, 86
Rakes, need in garden, 76
Rape, as green manure crop,
  43
Record-keeping. *See* Journal
Redwood, for cold frame
  construction, 94
Rhubarb, general growing
  tips for, 172–73
Rock phosphate, as natural
  fertilizer, 34–35
Rotation, of crops, for
  disease control, 66
Rototiller, need in garden,
  78
Rotovator, need in garden,
  78
Rutabaga, general growing
  tips for, 159–60
Rye, as green manure crop,
  43

S

Salad potatoes. *See* Potatoes,
  new
Salsify, general growing
  tips for, 223–24
Sanitation, for disease
  control, 66
Sawdust, as mulch material,
  56, 59
Scallion. *See* Onions

Scarlet runner beans, as
  cover crop, 44
Seaweed, 35
  as mulch material, 57,
  59
Seeder, need in garden, 78
Seeds, germination test, 82
  selection of, 82–83
Sets, onion, 132
Sewage sludge, as natural
  fertilizer, 36
Shallots, general growing
  tips for, 136
Sheep sorrel, use as
  beneficial weed, 70
Sheet composting, 57
Shrimp meal, as natural
  calcium source, 36
Side-dressing, of fertilizer,
  38
Sledgehammer, need in
  garden, 78
Slugs, control with wood
  ashes, 35
Snow peas. *See* Peas, edible-
  podded
Soaker hoses, for drip
  irrigation systems, 23
Soaking, of seeds, to ensure
  germination, 104
Sodium, need as trace
  mineral in soil, 29
Soil, fertilization of, 28–31,
  33–39
  humus in, 31–33
  pH of, 39–41
  trace minerals in, 29
  water loss from, 18, 54
Soil test, necessity of, 30
Solanine, produced by
  potatoes, 120

249

Index